MW01113624

established

Seeking God's Plan for Spiritual Growth

PAM PALAGYI

Established: Seeking God's Plan for Spiritual Growth

Copyright © 2015 Pam Palagyi

ISBN 978-1-945084-03-4

www.pampalagyi.com

Unless otherwise indicated, all Scripture quotations are taken from The Holy Bible, New International Version. Copyright © 1973,1978,1984 by International Bible Society.

Published by Arise Publishing

DEDICATION

I dedicate this book to seekers of truth...
May your journey begin with these pages.

They will be called oaks of righteousness, a
planting of the Lord for the display of his splendor.
Isaiah 61:3

TABLE OF CONTENTS

INTRODUCTION

Are you living an abundant life?

Have you asked yourself questions like...

Who am I and how do I relate to God?

Do I have a destiny, a God-directed plan for my life?

How can I overcome the daily obstacles and difficulties?

God created a perfect world. He planned for us to live a dynamic and fulfilled life within that realm. If your present lifestyle falls short of his best, then it is time to revisit the original design!

Established: Seeking God's Plan for Spiritual Growth unveils God's blueprint for success. When life began in the Garden of Eden, God provided five key elements essential to his plan. And you have a personal invitation to rediscover this garden!

As we enter the gate, we become part of his family, the family of God. At first glance we may resemble your own relatives. But if you look closely, we differ from one another. We are young and old, male and female, multi-colored, multi-national, and multi-racial. We live in grass-thatched huts as well as luxury penthouses. Our family stretches around the world, even in the most remote of places. Yet, we all hold tightly to one common truth—God sent his Son into the world to give us a special kind of life.

Our common belief in Jesus as the Son of God connects us as a unique family. We experienced a spiritual awakening because of Jesus, our Savior. We posses a universal, spiritual DNA which defines us a family.

You may ask, "What is a Savior and why do I need one?"

We live in a world filled with imperfections—imperfect people performing imperfect tasks in imperfect ways with imperfect thoughts and imperfect motivations getting imperfect results. And you dwell right in the middle of it!

God began with a different plan. He created a perfect world. When his intentions failed, he provided a means to overcome the results—the obstacles and difficulties we face on a daily basis. God designed a simple, yet powerful transaction called "salvation."

Each of us has the opportunity to trade our personal failures for his goodness. When you relinquish the pain and disappointments of life into his hands, you receive a spotless new beginning.

What a deal!

Your life changed for all of eternity.

As the first step in your new spiritual journey, you likely have questions that need answers. I did.

I approached God eager for answers. He did not flinch at my lack of understanding. In fact, he only desired that I come to him with an open heart and mind. He welcomes you to do the same.

How to Use This Book

Established fits many different settings and uses. First, it works for individual study. As a self-directed study, the sections present thought-provoking questions and scripture for personal reflection.

Small groups, Bible studies, new members classes, or one-on-one mentoring also benefit from the format. The questions can be used for personal reflection as well as further discussion and study.

If you seek answers to spiritual questions, *Established* provides answers. For new believers, the book lays a solid foundation in the Christian faith. Mature believers revisit the basic tenets of faith and revive their spiritual walk.

I pray that you would have an open mind and heart as you read these pages. God will direct your path in his truth.

Let's begin our spiritual journey!

Chapter 1

THE POWER OF CHOICE

In the classic movie *Indiana Jones and the Last Crusade*, the hero faces a critical decision. He must identify the genuine Holy Grail, the cup of Christ, from among several imitations. If he makes the right choice, a drink from the life-giving cup will save his dying father. The wrong one will be lethal.

Indiana wavers. Which cup is the right one? After a few moments, he rejects the golden goblets and instead grabs a plain, earthen cup. He dips the chalice into the water, puts it to his lips, and takes a sip. The medieval knight guarding the treasure affirms his selection, "You have chosen wisely!"

Decisions define and direct our lives.

Who do you date? What car will you buy? Which career path do you follow? Where should you live?

Life provides a selection of choices. Like Indiana's cups, some shimmer with a promise of fame and fortune. Others seem ordinary, almost boring.

Your countless choices have brought you to where you are today. They directed you along an unmarked pathway of your own making. Good ones positioned you for success. Poor ones brought disappointing results.

For many years I based my decisions on superficial qualities. Although my choices looked good on the surface, eventually they proved disastrous. I was left with a mess wondering how could I change.

And then I made one decision that changed my life forever. One moment in time arrested my roller-coaster ride and turned it into a journey of discovery.

A Moment of Decision

My story begins when my oldest daughter Lisa was in diapers and I was pregnant with my second child, Laurie. We moved hundreds of miles away from family and. I was overwhelmed at the thought of caring for two children. I could barely function with one little girl. How could I handle two?

Help arrived when a fiery redhead moved in across the street. Sandy was different from anyone I had ever met.

First, she always smiled. I could never figure out why!

Sandy had three rambunctious boys that were five, three, and one year old. They rushed through the house shrieking and yelling, slamming doors and stomping up and down the stairs. What a racket! The two older brothers teased their younger brother who reacted with blood-curdling screams and a dramatic overflow of tears. How could anyone smile in the midst of that?

The second thing unique about Sandy was her conversation. I was acquainted with God. I had watched a few Bible movies, attended Vacation Bible School, and even went to church on rare occasions. But she talked about God like she knew Him. Sandy spoke about God like He was her friend.

"Oh, God helped me make bread this morning. I forgot the salt and He reminded me to put it in."

What was that, Sandy?

"Yes, He helps me all the time. I can ask God a question and He gives me an answer. I don't know what I would do without Him!"

Sandy's concept of God differed from anything I had heard or experienced. She spoke about her relationship like He was her best friend...and He was! Sandy's God was not the unapproachable, remote deity in the heavens I had understood Him to be. He was a living, touchable Being who demonstrated His love for her on a daily basis. It sounded too good to be true. I was fascinated with the possibility of God as my friend!

One night, I was reading a book searching for answers in my "quest for truth." Suddenly, I sensed an unknown presence illuminating the words. The simple truth of the Gospel message radiated from the pages of the book. What was previously confusing suddenly became crystal clear.

For the first time I recognized the reality of Jesus Christ as the Son of God. I remember saying something like "God, this sounds right to me. If this is true then the rest of it must also be true. So, I believe in you Jesus. You are the Son of God."

I was changed the moment I uttered those words. Something inside of me transformed. The unanswered questions fled. I felt a lightness, a buoyancy, and freshness to life which was indescribable.

My decision was what many call being "born again." I experienced God's glorious power to remake a person from the inside out. At the age of twenty-nine, my journey with God began.

That initial decision was only the first of many I would make. I needed spiritual guidance, but where would I find it?

God was ready with answers. He had already provided a path for me to follow.

God Has a Plan for You!

When designing a home, an architect creates blueprints defining every detail in the structure. His draft consists of different viewpoint of the future home. Each level is detailed with the electrical outlets, floor dimensions, positioning of the windows, doors, plumbing and walls. The blueprint is intricate with details.

A builder must learn to read these plans and understand what each notation means. This ensures that the home will be built according to the architect's design. The concrete must be poured in the right dimensions, the framing plumb, and each wall, door, and window placed exactly where the drawing indicates. By following the blueprint, the builder creates a home that will be thoroughly enjoyed for many years.

God also has a master plan for all of Creation. He provided a design for a life in harmony with Him.

He has already engineered the foundation, planned for the framework, and worked out even the smallest of details. If we deviate from His original design, our lives become unbalanced, our emotions skewed, and our desires misaligned. The result is not an architect's dream, but an eyesore evident to everyone.

In order to avoid this faulty "do-it-yourself" building project, God provided guidelines to direct the work in progress. These spiritual principles keep it aligned properly with His design. They are found within the pages of the Bible, God's loving master plan for humanity. The Book of Proverbs says this:

> *It takes wisdom to build a house, and*
> *understanding to set it on a firm foundation;*
> *It takes knowledge to furnish its rooms*
> *with fine furniture and beautiful draperies.*
> *(Proverbs 24:3-4, The Message Bible)*

God has filled His manual with wisdom, knowledge and understanding for living a godly life. What manufacturer creates a product and does not include a handbook of instructions?

God's guidebook for successful living begins in Genesis, the very first book of the Bible. Here we discover God's original plan for mankind...his perfect blueprint for our life.

It Starts "In the Beginning..."

Genesis is the first book of the Bible, sometimes called "the book of beginnings." It opens with these words... *"In the beginning God created."*

For six days God spoke the world into being, rejoicing over His creative expression. (Genesis 1:10, 12, 21,

25, 31) From the fish that leaped from the waters to the gentle rustling of the breeze through the trees, He was thrilled to watch each creation. God saw what he had made and called it "good."

The world was complete except for one thing. God desired a reflection of His very essence. He wanted someone who would communicate and interact with Him. Therefore, as the culminating act in Genesis, He fashioned human beings:

> *Then God said, "Let us make man in our image, in our likeness...." So God created man in his own image, in the image of God he created him; male and female he created them. God blessed them (male and female) and said to them, "Be fruitful and increase in number; fill the earth and subdue it. Rule over the fish of the sea and the birds of the air and over every living creature that moves on the ground." (Genesis 1:26-28)*

God placed the crown of creation in the Garden of Eden. The male and female took care of the Garden and enjoyed daily fellowship with God. Their only restriction was:

> *"You are free to eat from any tree in the garden; but you must not eat from the tree of the knowledge of good and evil, for when you eat of it you will surely die." (Genesis 2:16-17)*

Mankind had ultimate liberty in the garden. Male and female were free to eat, work, play, and communicate with God and each other in a perfect environment. They possessed a divine identity. They were made in the image of God Himself. They exercised authority over all of God's creation.

In addition, male and female lived in community with each other and in relationship to God. He visited daily to talk with them in the garden. They walked out their destiny as they tended the garden of God and became stewards of His creation. Finally, God had provided for their every need. They experienced abundance straight from the hand of God; He was their sufficiency.

It was an ideal situation, a perfect design with only one restriction. Do not eat from the tree of the knowledge of good and evil! God warned them that this tree did not offer life, but the severe penalty of death.

Unfortunately, God's perfection came to an end. An evil presence in the form of a crafty serpent entered the garden. Deceiving the woman with lies, the cunning serpent interjected rebellion into God's creation. Both the woman and the man ate from the forbidden tree. God's perfect world changed:

> *When the woman saw that the fruit of the tree was good for food and pleasing to the eye, and*

*also desirable for gaining wisdom, she took some
and ate it. She also gave some to her husband,
who was with her, and he ate it. Then the eyes of
both of them were opened, and they realized they
were naked; so they sewed fig leaves together and
made coverings for themselves. (Genesis 3:1-7)*

Imperfection marred the glory of God's creation. In
His mercy, God could not allow them to live forever
in this flawed condition. He banished them from the
Garden of Eden and separated them from the source
of everlasting life. He positioned two angels at the
entrance of Eden preventing them from re-entering.
(Genesis 3:24)

One selfish decision altered His original plan for
humanity. Creation shifted into a shadow of its
former existence.

The Garden Revisited

How did God react when the male and female ruined
His carefully laid plans?

He could respond in a variety of ways. God might
throw up His hands in exasperation and quit, turning
away from the mess that lay before Him. He could
fume over Adam and Eve's selfish disobedience.
"Didn't I tell you not to eat from that tree! Now what
am I going to do?" He could sentence humanity to
eternal isolation and punishment.

Instead, a loving God responded with mercy!

The Creator realized humanity would not live in Eden forever. He knew their weakness and eventual failure, but proceeded with His plan. God stood at the brink of creation and peered into the future, past the fall of humanity, past the mistakes and pain of human existence, into a time when all things would be restored.

In the exact time and at the precise place, God sent His only Son Jesus to earth in the form of a human being.

Why?

So that we could be reconciled to our heavenly Father!

The breach between mankind and God that occurred in the Garden of Eden came to an end. God reached out towards creation once again. He sent his Son to draw humanity back to the original plan.

The compassionate heart of God beat in the chest of His son. Jesus walked the earth as a human being demonstrating what it meant to live a godly life. His perfect love, the magnificence of His glory, the generosity of His spirit, and the power of His divine strength beckoned humanity to return to God. He was an example of how to be connected to and empowered by a caring God:

The Word became flesh and blood, and moved into the neighborhood. We saw the glory with our own eyes, the one-of-a-kind glory, like Father, like Son, Generous inside and out, true from start to finish. (John 1:14, The Message Bible)

Jesus is called the second Adam in scripture. Where the first Adam chose rebellion and failed, the second Adam would triumph. Once again, God chose the site of a garden as the stage for His divine drama.

In the Garden of Gethsemane, Jesus Christ, the second Adam, faced a choice. Would he submit to his Father's plan for redeeming mankind? Knowing an agonizing death awaited his decision, His human nature struggled. Christ appealed to the Father with *"My Father, if it is possible, may this cup be taken from me. Yet not as I will, but as you will."* (Matthew 26:39)

Yet, Jesus submitted to death on a cross because there was a divine purpose to it. He looked through the terrible suffering and saw humanity restored. He witnessed the joy of men and women in right relationship with God. Jesus saw you and he saw me. His eyes focused on the ultimate goal of redemption and he endured for our sakes:

Let us fix our eyes on Jesus, the author and perfecter of our faith, who for the joy set before him endured the cross, scorning

> *its shame, and sat down at the right hand*
> *of the throne of God. (Hebrews 12:2)*

He, too, chose wisely.

You may be asking…why the blood? Why the cross? Couldn't God have invented some other plan?

God established a precedent in the Garden of Eden modeled throughout the Old Testament. When Adam and Eve sinned, they immediately felt the results. The covering of God lifted. Although they clothed themselves with fig leaves, their attempt failed.

God provided animal skins to hide their vulnerability He linked the sacrifice of an animal and its blood to the means of covering their sin.

The Old Testament used animal offerings to atone for wrongdoings. They foreshadowed the final, ultimate sacrifice of one human for all of mankind.

God's plan for salvation was simple, but extremely costly. Jesus was called the Lamb of God because he would be that final sacrifice. He bore the weight of humanity's wrongs upon Himself on the cross. Sin with its ugliness and deadly consequences ended. It was the last offering God would require.

A new agreement between God and humans began on that day. A single decision redeemed humanity. All disobedience, wrongdoing, and every violation against God were destroyed with Christ's death.

Mankind was set free:

> *He did not enter by means of the blood of goats and calves; but he entered the Most Holy Place once for all by his own blood, having obtained eternal redemption...How much more, then, will the blood of Christ, who through the eternal Spirit offered himself unblemished to God, cleanse our consciences from acts that lead to death, so that we may serve the living God! (Hebrews 9:12-14)*

And so the promise of life once made in the Garden of Eden is available again for all of mankind. God has reshaped the results of Adam's failure. Instead of guilt, condemnation and punishment, He offers the joy of relating to Him with a clean conscience. The second Adam, Jesus, paved the way!

> *For since death came through a man, the resurrection of the dead comes also through a man. For as in Adam all die, so in Christ all will be made alive. (1 Corinthians 15:21)*

Welcome Back to the Garden

Remember those two angels that were placed at the entrance to the Garden of Eden? Their mission prevented Adam and Eve from re-entering Eden in their flawed state. God refused to allow them to live forever in that condition.

These angels appear again as the guardians of God in his holy temple. A thick curtain hung in the area called the Holy of Holies. The two angelic beings were symbolically woven into the curtain that guarded the presence of God.

Only the high priest of Israel entered this area once a year. He carried the blood of a sacrificed animal with incense burning in a censer. The rest of the year, these angels shielded Israel from the presence of God. No one had access.

At the exact time when Christ died on the cross, that curtain with the angels woven into it was torn in two by an unseen hand. It was ripped from the top to bottom:

> *And when Jesus had cried out again in a loud voice, he gave up his spirit. At that moment the curtain of the temple was torn in two from top to bottom. (Matthew 27:50-51)*

The angels parted and the entrance to the Holy of Holies opened. God invited mankind back into His presence.

With the sacrifice of Christ and the tearing of the veil that separated humanity from God, we now experience the fullness of God's presence. Access into the Garden of Eden is available once again! God's original plan for humanity with all of its provisions and promises are waiting your return.

The path back into the Garden of Eden begins with believing Jesus is God's Son. This one decision will change your life forever. You are no longer an outsider beyond the gates of the garden.

The way is open…come on in!

God welcomes you into His special place of Creation. This garden, what Christians now call the Kingdom of God, has its own culture and its own godly perspectives.

In the following pages you will discover what it means to be a child of God, a creation of the Most High God. You will begin to realize your new identity, authority, community, destiny and sufficiency bought through the sacrifice of Jesus Christ.

Welcome to the Family of God!

If you are not sure of your salvation experience or want to recommit your life to God, repeat this simple prayer from your heart:

Jesus,

I believe you are the Son of God. I know you died on the cross for my sins. Please forgive me for my mistakes and wrong doings. I ask you for a fresh start and a new beginning. I choose to make you the Lord of my life.

Thank you, Jesus.

Amen

Chapter 2

DESTINY...A PLAN FOR GROWTH

On a cruise to Mexico, I joined a team that went ashore as part of a mission outreach. We prayed with the families and played with the precious children awaiting medical treatment.

As we relaxed under the shade of a cypress tree, I noticed a teenage girl translating for the medical staff. Her father lost his job in the United States and they were forced to return to Mexico. After being uprooted from the only home she had ever known, she resented her current situation. The young lady planned on moving back to the United States as soon as she turned eighteen.

During a break, I had an opportunity to chat and pray with her. As I was about to leave, I asked, "Do you know that God has a plan for your life?" Her big brown eyes were filled with tears and she stammered, "No, I didn't!"

Suddenly, her countenance changed and she began to smile. She wasn't isolated. Her situation was not hopeless. God had mapped out a course and she didn't need to stumble through life wondering where to live or what should she do. That one simple revelation radically changed her perspective. A newfound hope rose within her.

God also has a plan for your life!

You may have asked the same kind of questions. "Why am I here?" "What is my life all about?"

As humans, we are convinced our existence should be meaningful. We struggle to find ourselves through our occupation, finances, the clothes we wear, or the house we occupy. But when that fleeting sense of accomplishment fades, we can be left wondering, "Is that all there is?"

God has made you in a unique way. You have been fashioned so that you fit precisely into a grander scheme. Your nature, personality, gift and talents all point to a higher calling than a mere day-to-day existence.

In God's big picture, each of us is like a puzzle piece. We fit exactly into one place, one key position that adds a particular pattern to the overall picture. There is a reason God created you. It is a divine destiny that can and will be fulfilled only in God.

The Apostle Paul put it this way:

For we are God's workmanship, created in Christ Jesus to do good works, which God prepared in advance for us to do. (Ephesians 2:10)

God has a plan and you are part of it! When we discover what we have been created for, we find true significance in life. We find purpose.

When we direct our actions according to that revelation, we find a new measure of worth and meaning. That is destiny.

Destiny is God's divine intention for our life.

We each possess different strengths and talents. God designed our abilities for a certain objective...a goal, a life message and direction. Whatever our age or gender, God has a strategy to reach that purpose.

The Westminster Catechism, a traditional form of instruction in the Christian church, addresses destiny like this: *Find your purpose in God, fulfill it, and enjoy His company along the way.*

What a simple formula! If we discover why we have been created and stay connected to God,we fulfill that unique calling. Only then do we experience satisfaction and find great success!

God's Universal Plan for Growth

God's original purpose for mankind states: *God blessed them and said to them, "Be fruitful and increase in number; fill the earth and subdue it.* (Genesis 1:28)

Within his pristine world, God directed his male and female creation to grow, reproduce, fill and fulfill their godly assignment. They were to establish God's rule upon the earth. These four commands complete the universal assignment for humanity.

You might think "But that was easy for Adam and Eve! The earth was a blank sheet of paper!"

Let us approach these statements as directives given not only to the first humans, but to us as individuals. We can apply them to our life today.

Be Fruitful. Surrounded by an abundance of fruit trees that were *"pleasing to the eye and good for food"* (Genesis2:9), God told humanity to be fruitful. What kind of fruit could a human being bear?

Not apples or berries! No, this Hebrew word for "fruitful" is *parah* which means "to flourish, bear fruit, be abundant and *do not be a sucker vine!"*

I am a backyard gardener and understand what a sucker vine does, especially with regards to tomatoes.

As the central stalk thickens, branches jut out from all sides. Some have small yellow flowers that will eventually produce the juicy red tomatoes that I love. Other branches display dense green leaves, but the flowers are absent. Those non-fruit bearing branches divert nutrients and limit the tomato's ability to produce succulent red globes. Their foliage is attractive, but it drains the life and energy from the plant.

These branches are called "suckers." They enhance the look of the plant, but have no specific use. I pinch them off and redirect the energy of the tomato plant to its fruit-bearing limbs.

We are called to be fruitful, but it is easy to fall into the same "sucker vine" mentality. We scurry around, plunge ourselves into extra activities, only to end up exhausted. Like the tomato, our energy is directed towards non-fruitful branches.

Or maybe you have developed a "what is in it for me?" mindset. We become all leaves and show, but we are one-sided in our efforts. God intended that we would bear fruit and give back to the world in which we live.

Galatians 5:22 describes the internal spiritual fruit which God desires for us to grow: *But the fruit of the Spirit is love, joy, peace, patience, kindness, goodness, faithfulness, gentleness and self-control.* (Galatians 5:22)

As we mature in our Christian walk, we cultivate the nature of our Heavenly Father through our actions and words. We display our harvest of spiritual fruit when we bake cookies for our family, reach out to a hurting friend, or extend a helping hand to someone in need.

Like a living branch, we require occasional pruning. Trimming back the non-essential growth enables us to become even more productive. Jesus explained the pruning and fruit-bearing process to His disciples like this—remain in close relationship and you will bear fruit:

> *I (Jesus) am the Real Vine and my Father is the Farmer. He cuts off every branch of me that doesn't bear grapes. And every branch that is grape-bearing he prunes back so it will bear even more...Live in me. Make your home in me just as I do in you. In the same way that a branch can't bear grapes by itself but only by being joined to the vine, you can't bear fruit unless you are joined with me...I am the Vine, you are the branches. When you're joined with me and I with you, the relation intimate and organic, the harvest is sure to be abundant. (John 15:1-5, The Message Bible)*

Finally, in order to bear fruit we must dwell in a nurturing environment. All natural vegetation requires sunlight to grow. Light is necessary for photosynthesis. We also need spiritual light to come to maturity.

A simple science experiment demonstrates how important light is for growth. In elementary school, our class cultivated several bean plants. We chose one and stuck it in a dark closet for a few days. When it was removed, the stalk had turned from brilliant green to a sickly yellow. The leaves drooped. The robust plant became unhealthy because the environment was inappropriate. The bean plant required sunlight for growth.

In a similar way, God has called us to walk in the light with Him and avoid the dark influences of this world. We need a full measure of His radiance in order to be fruitful:

> *For you were once darkness, but now*
> *you are light in the Lord. Live as children of*
> *light (for the fruit of the light consists in all*
> *goodness, righteousness and truth) and find*
> *out what pleases the Lord. Have nothing to*
> *do with the fruitless deeds of darkness, but*
> *rather expose them. (Ephesians 5:8-11)*

Increase in Number. In Genesis 1:28, the second command of God is to "increase in number." The Hebrew word is *raba...* "to grow great, increase, to become numerous, enlarge, and increase in status."

God is not stagnant. He is not passive or sterile. He does not expect his children to be! We are instructed to be dynamic, expanding within and without as examples of his goodness.

From the very beginning, God created us with the inherent ability to reproduce, both physically and spiritually. The obvious response is physical reproduction. Adam and Eve would give birth to Cain, Abel, and Seth. Their offspring would populate the earth fulfilling this portion of God's directive.

We are also called to reproduce spiritually. The final words Jesus spoke to his disciples was wait for the promise of the Holy Spirit. He would give them *"power to become His witnesses on earth." (Acts 1:8)*

The parting words directed his disciples to *go and make disciples of all nations… and teaching them to obey everything I have commanded you.* (Matthew 28:19-20) We are representatives of Christ's kingdom. Like the first disciples, we are given a ministry on earth to be the carriers of the gospel message:

> *God has given us the task of telling everyone what he is doing. We're Christ's representatives. God uses us to persuade men and women to drop their differences and enter into God's work of making things right between them. We're speaking for Christ himself now: Become friends with God; he's already a friend with you. (2 Corinthians 5:18-20, The Message Bible)*

Therefore, part of our destiny involves sharing the good news about Jesus Christ.

What has he done in your life?

How have you changed?

This is your testimony of God's goodness expressed toward you. Will you stand on a street corner and shout the message of salvation? A few do, but generally your testimony will be shared as one-on-one encounters with friends, colleagues, and sometimes strangers as they cross your path. We should be ready whenever the opportunity arises.

I learned this lesson firsthand after a mission trip to the Philippines. I climbed on the plane exhausted after thirteen days of mission work. My team spent a sleepless night sailing across the channel between islands. All I wanted to do was close my eyes and rest on the flight to Hong Kong. However, God had something else in mind.

A talkative French-Canadian physicist sat down next to me on the plane. Although I was tired, I grudgingly began to have a conversation with him. As I shared my recent activities on the mission field, he spoke of his dissatisfaction with religion. This scientist had grown up in a religious environment, even considered the priesthood at one point, but had never really connected to God.

I made one statement which grabbed his attention. I merely said, "Christ is not a religion. He is a relationship."

As we continued our friendly chat, I realized this was a divine appointment set up by God. When I asked if he knew Jesus on a personal level, he answered honestly, "I don't know."

My answer was, "Would you like to?" and he smiled and said, "Yes!"

That led to his life-changing prayer at 30,000 feet above the Pacific Ocean. It was a perfect end to my mission trip to the Philippines!

We can each look to Jesus as our example for growth and increase. He taught the principles of sowing a seed and reaping a harvest (Galatians 6:7-9), showed His disciples where to catch an abundance of fish (Luke 5:4-7, John 21:6), and multiplied a few loaves of bread and fish into a feast for thousands (Matthew 14:19).

With the anointing of God resting upon Him, Jesus caused all things to expand and thrive. And just like Jesus, we too, have ability beyond our natural limits. The power of God to increase rests on our lives.

Fill the Earth. The third command during creation was to "fill the earth." The Hebrew word "fill" is *male,* "to fill, fulfill, satisfy, accomplish, be completed."

Creation was the first step for God. He anticipated expansion, completion, and fulfillment. He began the work, set it in motion, but invited humans to co-labor with him. His goal was a populated, saturated earth teeming with life.

The same holds true for our individual lives. We come into the world full of promise. We are like a blank canvas waiting to be painted. The colors are selected, the brushes are ready, but the picture will take decades to paint. The Master artist is not in a hurry! Every inch of the canvas will be covered, every brush stroke finished with a flourish.

We have a lifetime to fulfill the divine destiny given to each of us.

Completion.

Fulfillment.

Satisfaction.

That's what the words "fill the earth" point to. God wants us to be whole—full of His Spirit, full of His life, full of His promise. Do you have longings that yearn for expression and completion?

Keep going. It is never too late! At the age of forty-five, I went back to school and earned a Master of Divinity degree.

My friend Joyce was a British war bride. She married

young and came to live in New England with her new husband. Joyce had always wanted to earn a college degree and in her sixties she went back to school. She graduated at the mature, yet fulfilled age of seventy-five!

Move forward in faith and step up to a greater level of spiritual maturity. You may not have arrived, but as the Apostle Paul states, continue to press on:

> *Not that I have already obtained all this, or have already been made perfect, but I press on to take hold of that for which Christ Jesus took hold of me. Brothers, I do not consider myself yet to have taken hold of it. But one thing I do: Forgetting what is behind and straining toward what is ahead, I press on toward the goal to win the prize for which God has called me heavenward in Christ Jesus. (Philippians 3:12-14)*

Subdue It. As caretakers in the garden, Adam and Eve exercised authority and brought God's rule and ways into the garden: *The Lord God took the man and put him in the Garden of Eden to <u>work</u> it and <u>take care</u> of it. (Genesis 2:15)*

Man was to cultivate the land, serve it, guard, and preserve it. He was called to the ongoing task of stewardship over God's creation.

The Hebrew word for subdue is *kabash,* "to overcome, control, conquer and control an environment." Like

Adam and Eve, we too have a divine assignment. God places us within a physical realm and gives us a time frame for completion:

> *From one man he made every nation of men, that they should inhabit the whole earth; and he determined the times set for them and the exact places where they should live. (Acts 17:26)*

"Sphere of influence" is a term which defines your place of authority. Where do you have influence? Whose lives do you touch on a regular basis? Your sphere may be a household, a neighborhood, or the workplace. The average person will affect over six thousand people during their life! Who and what is in your world?

Remember the Lord's Prayer..."*Your kingdom come, Your will be done?*" These are not idle words, but a personal calling to bring God's will to pass on the earth.

What is His will in your "sphere of influence?"

Because we carry the nature of God, we can begin to establish a godly atmosphere by our presence alone. We intervene with prayer, calling forth the presence of God as a continual influence. The authority of God can transform our surroundings.

Be fruitful and increase in number; fill the earth and subdue it. These four were God's first assignments

41

for humanity, and yet, they are still applicable to us today. As children of God, we grow, increase, accomplish God's will, and establish His rule on the earth.

Finding Your Destiny

How do we discover our destiny?

Begin by taking an inventory. What are your strengths? They may include a tangible skill like the ability to strum a guitar and sing. Or your specialty may be something more intangible like compassion or generosity.

When God created you, He molded various traits into the fabric of your being. They distinguish who you are. Only in Christ do we find the fulfillment of that destiny:

It's in Christ that we find out who we are and what we are living for. Long before we first heard of Christ and got our hopes up, he had his eye on us, had designs on us for glorious living, part of the overall purpose he is working out in everything and everyone. (Ephesians 1:11, The Message Bible)

As you begin to pray and ask God to reveal his plan for your life, ask in faith. Believe He not only wants to answer, but He will:

If you don't know what you're doing, pray to the Father. He loves to help. You'll get his help, and won't be condescended to when you ask for it. Ask boldly, believingly, without a second thought. (James 1:5, The Message Bible)

Don't be afraid to step out and try something new! God doesn't always look for the most qualified, or the highly educated, the gorgeous, or the rich. He finds the ordinary and makes them extraordinary. He chooses the common and uses them in uncommon ways.

Your destiny may be bigger than your circumstances!

In the Bible, a man named Abraham was destined to be the father of many nations. However, he was childless. His wife Sarah was barren.

Yet, God gave Abraham a promise, a destiny beyond his natural ability to attain it. Faith was the key that unlocked Abraham's destiny. Abraham's faith rested in a God who could perform whatever was necessary to fulfill his call.

Abraham believed God. The One who had promised him a family would bring it to pass:

We call Abraham "father" not because he got God's attention by living like a saint, but because God made something out of Abraham when he was a nobody...When everything was hopeless, Abraham believed anyway, deciding to live not on the basis of what he saw he couldn't do but on what God said he would do...Abraham didn't focus on his own impotence and say, "It's hopeless. This hundred-year-old body could never father a child." Nor did he survey Sarah's decades of infertility and give up. He didn't tiptoe around God's promise asking cautiously skeptical questions. He plunged into the promise and came up strong, ready for God, sure that God would make good on what he had said. (Romans 4:17-21, The Message Bible)

An Israelite named David was destined to be King of Israel. He was a young shepherd boy stuck out in the fields with a bunch of smelly sheep. His own father ignored him when the prophet Samuel came to visit. David was summoned to join the family as an afterthought.

But God saw something different in David. He directed Samuel to anoint David as the next king of Israel. This shepherd-king would slay the giant Goliath, overrun the Philistine enemy, and become the greatest ruler Israel would ever know. (1 Samuel)

Joseph's story began when his brothers sold him into slavery. He was falsely accused and sent to prison. But Joseph became the prime minister of Egypt during a time of famine. He saved the nation of Egypt and Israel from starvation (Genesis 37-50).

Esther was an orphan in a foreign country, but she was destined to become queen and save her people from destruction (Esther). Deborah was a woman filled with wisdom who led her nation to victory over its enemy (Judges 4-5).

The Apostle Paul was the least likely candidate to be chosen as a minister of God. Paul was a zealot, persecuting the church. His religious fervor led him to take part in the stoning of Stephen, the first Christian martyr.

But God had a plan for Paul.

On the road to Damascus, Paul met the Lord Jesus in a startling way (Acts 9). Knocked down and blinded by a brilliant light, Paul came face-to-face with Jesus. God transformed his life.

Paul had a destiny in God, and even though he had run very hard in the wrong direction, God redirected and equipped him for the life he was meant to live. Paul the persecutor became Paul the preacher.

At the end of his life, the Apostle Paul knew he had accomplished his earthly assignment. He traveled the Roman world preaching and teaching the gospel message. He established many churches in the name of Christ and helped birth the early church.

When death came knocking at his door. Paul knew he had run his race. He had finished those things which God had placed in his heart to do:

For I am already being poured out like a drink offering, and the time has come for my departure. I have fought the good fight, I have finished the race, I have kept the faith. Now there is in store for me the crown of righteousness, which the Lord, the righteous Judge, will award to me on that day—and not only to me, but also to all who have longed for his appearing. (2 Timothy 4:6-8)

Paul had a divine destiny, a purpose to fulfill in God's far-reaching plan for humanity. God made sure he accomplished it.

The Bible is filled with nondescript men and women who had a divine destiny. God hasn't changed his game plan. He still calls, positions, and equips men and women. We can choose to go our own way and do whatever seems right in our own eyes, but there remains a greater design waiting to be realized.

God does not play favorites. He has a plan for you, too!

You may already follow his plan or you may discover that you have veered off the path. Maybe you did not know there was a plan. Wherever you are, God is able to redirect and recreate the course of your life.

Chapter 3

IDENTITY...PUTTING DOWN ROOTS

In God's kingdom, we are free to pursue his plans and fulfill our divine potential. But sometimes, in spite of his best intentions, we may still be experiencing what I call the "baby elephant syndrome."

When an elephant is young, a trainer must prepare the wild baby elephant to live as a domesticated beast. In order to accomplish this, the trainer attaches a sturdy metal band around the elephant's foot and chains him to a stake in the ground. The chain confines the baby to a specified area and no matter how hard the baby elephant tries, he cannot get free. He pulls to the left, he strains to the right, back and forth, back and forth, but he is no match for the restraint. In defeat, the baby elephant finally submits to the limits placed upon him and ceases to fight.

When the elephant matures, he finally possesses the strength to break free from the stake and chain. But he remembers the hopeless struggles of his youth and sees himself as a baby elephant restricted by infantile ability. The mature elephant lives a life chained to a stake. He could easily uproot the spike with a single thrust of his leg.

If he ever realized he was a strong, mature elephant, he could easily break free.

Do you ever feel like that baby elephant?

What is holding you back?

In Christ, we are a *new creation; the old has gone, the new has come!* (2 Corinthians 5:17) We can shake off the old restraints and find the freedom that Christ purchased for us on the cross. The Apostle Paul wrote this to the church in Rome:

> *Don't become so well-adjusted to your culture that you fit into it without even thinking. Instead, fix your attention on God. You'll be changed from the inside out. Readily recognize what he wants from you, and quickly respond to it. Unlike the culture around you, always dragging you down to its level of immaturity, God brings the best out of you, develops well-formed maturity in you. (Romans 12:2, The Message Bible)*

What does God say about you?

What is his masterful design?

We can no longer afford to have a baby elephant's state of mind when the truth is right before us. The word of God is able to give us a fresh perspective, so that we, like the mature elephant, can break free.

Created in the Image of God

With a great sense of imagination and a touch of humor, God fashioned the animal kingdom. He created fur and feathers, bills and beaks, hooves and scales. It all pleased God and he *saw that it was good.* (Genesis 1:25) In one final crescendo of creativity, God created man:

> *So God created man in his own image,*
> *in the image of God he created him; male*
> *and female he created them.... God blessed*
> *them... God saw all that he had made, and it*
> *was very good...(Genesis 1:27, 28, 31)*

The Creator used words to make the natural world, but he crafted man with his hands. God became intimately involved with the formation of the human race:

> *...the Lord God formed the man from*
> *the dust of the ground and breathed into*

*his nostrils the breath of life, and the man
became a living being. (Genesis 2:7)*

Imagine, the Creator bending down to fashion the dust of the earth into a physical likeness of himself and then, softly breathing his life into that creation. Humanity came alive with the tender touch and kiss of God.

God planted his nature deep within Adam. Man had emotions, and intellect. He possessed the ability to choose, reason, and rule. He named the animals, tended the Garden of Eden, and functioned as a divine representative on earth. God fashioned man to walk, talk, act, and speak like him.

But something was still missing. God expressed his one note of displeasure over Creation with a simple declaration: *The Lord God said, "It is not good for the man to be alone. I will make a helper suitable for him."*(Genesis 2:18) The male needed an earthly companion to share his world.

God removed a rib from the male and refashioned it into something new. He created a companion, one who would be equal to the male and walk alongside him. The Hebrew words for "suitable helper" in Genesis 2:18 are *neged ezer*, which means "counterpart, opposite, or in close proximity to."

When Adam first looked upon this wonderful and fascinating being, he responded with:

50

> *The man said, "This is now bone of my*
> *bones and flesh of my flesh; she shall be called*
> *'woman,' for she was taken out of man." For*
> *this reason a man will leave his father and*
> *mother and be united to his wife, and they*
> *will become one flesh. (Genesis 2:23-2)*

One flesh. Together they represented the full, original image of mankind. Neither claimed the entirety of God's nature, but each had their exclusive part of God's image. The two complete the "one flesh" of the original creation.

Life in the garden sparkled with perfection: perfect love, perfect relationship, and perfect identity. They did not suffer with an inferiority complex or struggle with shame. Completely naked, the male and female did not think about cellulite dimples or droopy body parts!

And then they disobeyed and damaged their precious identity.

Adam and Eve felt the change. The glorious representation of God within them dimmed; sin took hold. It would take the strength and confidence of another to restore the divine image to the human race.

Christ, the Image of God

When Christ came to earth in the flesh, He did not

come as a talking chimpanzee, or a horse, or camel. He came as a human being. Just like the first Adam, he was made in the image and nature of his heavenly Father: *He is the image of the invisible God, the firstborn over all creation.* (Colossians 1:15)

The resemblance between Jesus and the Father was remarkable. The disciple Thomas asked Jesus to show him the Father and Jesus' response was, *Anyone who has seen me has seen the Father.* (John 14:9)

During his life on earth, Jesus made some startling statements about himself and that relationship. He presented a true image of his Father and a standard for his disciples to follow in every instance:

• Jesus acknowledged he could do nothing on his own. His actions mirrored only what he saw the Father doing:

I (Jesus) tell you the truth, the Son can do nothing by himself; he can do only what he sees his Father doing, because whatever the Father does the Son also does. (John 5:19)

• Jesus spoke only those words that the Father gave him to say. He clung to his Father's words and stayed true to his mission:

They did not understand that he was telling them about his Father. So Jesus said, "When

*you have lifted up the Son of Man, then you will
know that I am the one I claim to be and that I
do nothing on my own but speak just what the
Father has taught me. (John 8:27-28)*

• Jesus had the mind of God. He thought his
Father's thoughts and reasoned with divine
intellect:

*My purpose is that they may be encouraged in
heart and united in love, so that they may have
the full riches of complete understanding, in order
that they may know the mystery of God, namely,
Christ in whom are hidden all the treasures of
wisdom and knowledge. (Colossians 2:2-3)*

Jesus was the image and identity of the Father. He
was...*the radiance of God's glory and the exact
representation of his being.* (Hebrews 1:3) We now
have an example, a mirror to gaze into. Jesus became
the standard we follow to find our divine identity.

Made in His Image

Our divine identity is composed of two components:
a physical image and a spiritual inheritance. The
natural physical connection originates with our
earthly ancestor, Adam. The spiritual deposit within
us comes from our divine forerunner, Jesus:

And just as we have borne the likeness of the earthly man, so shall we bear the likeness of the man from heaven. (1 Corinthians 15:49)

Physical Connections. We have inherited a natural physical nature that is similar to the original design in the Garden of Eden. We are made in the image of God. These characteristics have been transferred from generation to generation. Humans have two arms, two feet, a mouth, nose, ears, and hair. We are able to make decisions and speak. Through Adam, we enjoy a universal likeness to God's original design.

In addition, God created each of us with a special blend of characteristics that represents a unique part of Him. We may all have hair, but some of us are blond, others brunette, and some red-headed! We are tall and short; our skin may be some shade of flesh-tone; our eyes could be blue, green, brown, or hazel. We are a reflection of a specific genetic code passed down through our particular ancestors. Yet, all of these traits are traceable back to the original male and female who possessed each of them within their physical make-up. We each represent a unique expression of God's handiwork:

For you created my inmost being; you knit me together in my mother's womb. I praise you because I am fearfully and wonderfully made; your works are wonderful, I know that full well. (Psalm 139:13-14)

Spiritual Connections. Our identity also contains a spiritual dimension. When we accept Jesus as our personal Savior, our spirit is born again. We receive the same life that God breathed into Adam and become a living, spiritual being:

> *For you have been born again, not of perishable seed, but of imperishable, through the living and enduring word of God. (1 Peter 1:23)*

Our new identity re-establishes God's divine nature in its original form. Salvation releases the power of transformation with God acting as that change agent. The sudden shift can be exhilarating, but it is only the first step in a process called "sanctification." This word simply means to "change by the divine power of God."

Sanctification is immediate when we pray and invite God into our lives, but it is also takes place over time. God's call to each believer is to become more like His Son. In our own strength, that task is impossible, but with God, all things are possible!

I was twenty-nine when I accepted Christ as my Savior. Amazingly, certain bad habits disappeared immediately when I accepted Christ. The new nature in Christ broke the power of sin and the effects were instant. However, it took time to mold other parts of my character. A few demanded outright effort on my part…and the process continues!

We never arrive at perfection in this world. Instead, God continues to transform us from within. He is erasing the old habits of our former self and establishing the divine nature of Christ:

> *Since, then, we do not have the excuse of ignorance, everything—and I do mean everything— connected with that old way of life has to go. It's rotten through and through. Get rid of it! And then take on an entirely new way of life—a God-fashioned life, a life renewed from the inside and working itself into your conduct as God accurately reproduces his character in you. (Ephesians 4:22-24, The Message Bible)*

A Healthy Identity

Where are you today? Do you find yourself struggling with a damaged identity because of the past? Whatever your current condition, Jesus Christ has the ability to redesign, restore, and renew your life.

The book of Proverbs states, *what he thinks is what he really is.* (Proverbs 23:7 GNT) If what we think about ourselves becomes our own reality, then the question remains, "What have we thought?" or better yet, "What have we been conditioned to think?"

According to psychology, three basic components form a healthy self-image. First, there is the need for **affection**. We long to know "I am loved." Love anchors us and allows us to mature while feeling secure in our environment.

Second, every human being longs for **acceptance**. We want to know that whoever we are, whatever God has created us to be, we are received. Being accepted in the family unit, the church, and community all contribute to our personal sense of well being.

Third, every man, woman, and child desires **affirmation** in order to develop a feeling of worth. We realize that who we are and what we do is acknowledged and appreciated.

These three are the root system for a balanced sense of worth, but few among us experience a full measure of affection, acceptance, and appreciation. As adults, we are flawed. We still thirst for the basics that were lacking in our upbringing.

Outside factors also contribute to the complex image that we have of ourselves: family, environment, as well as those specific experiences that are unique to each of us. Our identity is like wet cement. It is open to hand prints and stray dog tracks trailing across the surface which harden with time.

Culture also plays a role in our developing identity. Many countries promote personal freedom and opportunity. Other regions of the globe restrict their people because of social stigmas reinforced by the culture.

These binding restraints are tied to gender, economic strata, tribal origin, birth order, parentage, religion, or just being born on "the wrong side of the tracks." Women are considered second-class citizens in many parts of the world. Wealth, titles, and parental heritage become a distinguishing factor. Even skin color determines a person's worth.

Consider the caste system of India and how it confined men and women to certain positions in the social strata. By their very nature, castes defined a person's potential and worth. They dictated one's occupation, dietary habits, and interaction with members of other castes.

I have traveled to European nations where "the tall poppy" rule flourishes. In these countries, it is frowned upon to excel above others. If anyone rises higher than their core group or becomes a "taller poppy," they are cut down by their peers. All poppies have to remain at the same height!

In my case, I struggled with a warped identity that was anchored on physical beauty and appearance. My mother placed a high value on these attributes. I spent years struggling with feelings of inferiority and considered myself less desirable than those more physically attractive. This false standard affected my self-esteem and undermined my ability to become the woman God designed me to be.

In order to change, I had to discover a new perspective, a fresh point of reference different from my family's ideas. Trapped in a value system that produced constant frustration and failure, I had to discover God's standard that redefined me in a new and rewarding way: *Charm is deceptive, and beauty is fleeting; but a woman who fears the Lord is to be praised.* (Proverbs 31:30)

God's truth set me free from an unhealthy lie that plagued me from my youth. I learned that God values the internal, not the external. He looks at us from an eternal perspective and not a temporary one.

God Expresses His Love

As a human, Jesus was subject to the same basic needs that we experience today. God expressed all three...affection, acceptance and affirmation... towards his Son in one moment of time. When John the Baptist immersed Jesus in the Jordan River, the heavens opened up and Father's voice was heard:

At that time Jesus came from Nazareth in Galilee and was baptized by John in the Jordan. As Jesus was coming up out of the water, he saw heaven being torn open and the Spirit descending on him like a dove. And a voice came from heaven: "You are my Son, whom I love; with you I am well pleased." (Mark 1:9-11)

God expressed his love for Jesus. He boldly and publicly declared his affection, acceptance, and affirmation towards Christ. And here is the amazing thing...Jesus had not performed one miracle, healed the sick, or obediently gone to the cross.

God's, affection, acceptance, and affirmation were not connected to works. He reaffirmed Christ's identity because of love. There was no apology for the boasting of a proud Father God over his Son. His affection, acceptance, and affirmation were openly evident.

And here is the amazing thing...He feels the same way about you and me! You are loved. You are accepted. You are affirmed by God right where you are. If you lacked these things during your formative years or need a little extra assurance now and then, God is able to express them to you in a very personal manner.

The beauty of a Christian life is the ongoing revelation of God's care and devotion to each one of us. You no longer need to wonder who you are...you are His!

Dear God,

Thank you for loving me and creating me in your image. I believe you love me, accept me, and approve of me just how I am.

I choose to let go of the past...all of its hurts, pain, and disappointments. I believe that you are now working in me to become the person you designed me to be. I ask you to transform me and make me more like Jesus.

Thank you, God.

Amen

Chapter 4
AUTHORITY...FORTIFIED FAITH

Traffic jams...the curse of modern transportation! As officers direct traffic at an intersection, they restrict the movement of vehicles with a flick of their hand and a blast from their whistle. Police stand fearlessly in the midst of honking horns, weighty machinery, and disgruntled passengers.

And the drivers of the automobiles actually obey their commands!

One lane of cars moves through the intersection while another remains at a standstill. Despite the fact that the police officers could not physically stop an automobile, they stand at the crossroads with unwavering faith. They know the drivers will obey.

Every officer on duty does not act on his own. He or she serves as a representative of the government. Each has been given jurisdiction and commands the right to rule in that area. The government they represent empowers their actions and backs their decisions. It entrusts that right to the police force.

If a driver exceeds the speed limit, police do not travel to City Hall and find the mayor. No, they have been given the right to act in behalf of the city government. The officer issues the ticket. He does not summon the governor when placing handcuffs on a thief. The arresting officer has that duty.

That is authority.

The definition of authority is the "right and privilege" to take action. In Biblical Greek, the word for authority is *exousia*, meaning "the actual and unimpeded right to act, or to possess, control, use or dispose of, something or somebody."

Power differs from authority. Power is the ability or strength to accomplish an act. For example, the police officer does not have the power to stop a two-ton pickup truck. An officer would be killed instantly in a head-to-head collision with a truck. But they do command the "right" or authority to stop any vehicle because of their position in the governmental structure.

Similarly, the God of all power and authority gave

human beings the right and privilege to rule on earth. In the Garden of Eden, the male and female not only looked like God, but they also had been given the ability to act like him. According to God's directives found in Genesis, they had power, control, and dominion over God's creation:

> *God blessed them and said to them, "Be fruitful and increase in number; fill the earth and subdue it. Rule over the fish of the sea and the birds of the air and over every living creature that moves on the ground." Then God said, "I give you every seed-bearing plant on the face of the whole earth and every tree that has fruit with seed in it. They will be yours for food. (Genesis 1:28-30)*

Authority and power combine to represent one component of our godly mandate, "to subdue." Adam and Eve received that unique dispensation when they were created by God. They ruled over the garden where God had placed them.

In Genesis 2:15 we read: *God took the man and placed him into the Garden of Eden to work it and take care of it.* The word *shamar* is the Hebrew word for "take care of" and is also translated "to preserve, heed, watch over, guard, retain, and secure." God did not command Adam and Eve to perform a task and not equip them for the job. He gave them dominion in the midst of the garden.

Adam first exercised his authority when he named each of the animals God created. Imagine his excitement and joy as each of the peculiar creatures paraded before him! By naming each beast, he exercised his intellect, imagination, and dominion over them.

Now the Lord God had formed out of the ground all the beasts of the field and all the birds of the air. He brought them to the man to see what he would name them; and whatever the man called each living creature, that was its name. So the man gave names to all the livestock, the birds of the air and all the beasts of the field. (Genesis 2:19-20)

The male and female tended the Garden of Eden as emissaries of God. They were stewards of the garden and its inhabitants. Then they ate from the tree of knowledge of good and evil. (Genesis 3:6)

The consequences of this action included the loss of authority over God's creation. In essence, they handed over their rule and placed it in the hands of another, the one who had deceived them. Man would endure hardship, suffering, and bondage before the One would take back the precious gift that had been stolen.

The Authority of Christ

One Spring, my family and I toured England enjoying

the countryside and its many historic castles. The most memorable part for me was the Tower of London, and especially the Crown Jewels. Reserved for the coronation ceremony of each monarch, the Crown Jewels represent the sovereignty, majesty, and authority of that ruler over Great Britain.

At every coronation ceremony, these jeweled pieces are used as symbols of the new monarch's authority in the British realm. The Imperial Crown is placed on the royal's head to signify the power, legitimacy, and triumph of their position. The Sovereign's Orb represents the monarch's role as defender of the faith. The Scepter with the Cross represents kingly power and justice, and the Scepter with the Dove reflects the Holy Spirit, his equity, and mercy. These elements are physical representations of the monarch's power and authority. They are indicators of their right to rule.

In contrast to this lavish display in Great Britain, the King of Kings walked this earth without any outward signs of his rule. He did not wear a crown. Neither did he wave a golden scepter. Instead, Jesus came in humility and appeared as a common man.

How would anyone acknowledge his supreme power over all things? Who would accept his spiritual right to rule?

Christ's authority would not be recognized by jewelry

or robes. Instead, his claim to the throne of heaven would be proven by irrefutable demonstrations of power. From the baptism at the Jordan River until the close of his earthly life, Jesus confirmed that he had been given power and authority over all things.

After his baptism, Jesus was driven into the wilderness for forty days of fasting. In this desert arena, Jesus confronted Satan, the very one who had seized the authority from Adam. Jesus was challenged three times by his enemy. He countered the attack with truth from the Bible. Unlike Adam, who yielded to temptation when it arose, Jesus defeated his enemy in the desert with, "it is written:"

> *Then Jesus was led by the Spirit into the desert to be tempted by the devil. After fasting forty days and forty nights, he was hungry. The tempter came to him and said, "If you are the Son of God, tell these stones to become bread." Jesus answered, "**It is written**: 'Man does not live on bread alone, but on every word that comes from the mouth of God.'*

> *Then the devil took him to the holy city and had him stand on the highest point of the temple. "If you are the Son of God," he said, "throw yourself down. For it is written: "'He will command his angels concerning you, and they will lift you up in their hands, so that you will not strike your foot against a stone."*

*Jesus answered him, "**It is also written**: 'Do not put the Lord your God to the test.' "*

Again, the devil took him to a very high mountain and showed him all the kingdoms of the world and their splendor. "All this I will give you," he said, "if you will bow down and worship me."

*Jesus said to him, "Away from me, Satan! For **it is written**: 'Worship the Lord your God, and serve him only.' " Then the devil left him, and angels came and attended him. (Matthew 4:1-11)*

The religious leaders from Jerusalem also questioned Jesus about his authority. In that day, rabbis were expected to study with recognized scholars in preparation to teach. These religious leaders wanted to know where Jesus had received his formal education. In other words, what were His credentials for teaching in the temple? Was he actually qualified to speak to the crowds of people?

Christ's authority to teach and lead did not come from religious training. Instead, His authority came from heaven itself:

When Jesus had finished saying these things, the crowds were amazed at his teaching, because he taught as one who had authority, and not as their teachers of the law. (Matthew 7:28-29)

Jesus Christ openly displayed his power and authority through miracles and deliverance. He demonstrated his influence over the natural elements by commanding the fish of the sea (Luke 5:4-6), calming the raging storm (Luke 8:22-25), and walking on water (Matthew 14:25-27).

Countless times Jesus showed his superiority over demonic spirits and made them obey his every command. (Matthew 7:14-18, Mark 1:27) He healed the sick (Matthew 4:23), raised the dead (John 11:38-44), forgave sins (Luke 5:24), and claimed the power to judge. (John 5:27) His parting words to his disciples were, *All authority in heaven and on earth has been given to me.* (Matthew 28:18)

What a statement! Everything in creation, both in heaven and on the earth, came under the jurisdiction of Christ. What Adam lost in the garden, Christ recovered. With his final victory on the cross, Jesus conquered the evil of this world with one sacrificial act:

All sins forgiven, the slate wiped clean, that old arrest warrant canceled and nailed to Christ's Cross. He stripped all the spiritual tyrants in the universe of their sham authority at the Cross and marched them naked through the streets. (Colossians 2:13-15, The Message Bible)

The Greek word for "stripped" in this scripture is

apekduomai literally meaning "to separate, disrobe, and strip oneself", much like taking off a garment. Jesus shed all evil power and its influence like shrugging off a coat. And he did not stop there.

Whenever Roman generals would triumph in battle, it was customary to lead a procession of captives through the streets of Rome. In this way, they displayed the magnitude of their victory. This scripture tells us Christ shook off the enemy's influence. Then he organized a spiritual victory march to display his triumph over evil. He defeated every force of darkness!

Jesus Christ is the name that is greater than any name. He rules on high with complete confidence and assurance that the battle has been won. Jesus purchased the victory once and for all throughout eternity. He sits forever in the place of power and authority at the side of His Heavenly Father:

That power is like the working of his mighty strength, which he exerted in Christ when he raised him from the dead and seated him at his right hand in the heavenly realms, far above all rule and authority, power and dominion, and every title that can be given, not only in the present age but also in the one to come. And God placed all things under his feet and appointed him to be head over everything for the church, which is his body, the fullness of him who fills everything in every way. (Ephesians 1:18-23)

The Strength of the Believer: His Authority in Us

We know that Adam ruled in the Garden of Eden but lost his authority. Christ regained that authority and is now seated at the right hand of the Father. But what relevance does that have for us who still live here on earth?

The Book of Ephesians 1:3 states that we have *been blessed in the heavenly realms with every kind of spiritual blessing.* We are his children and have been positioned beside him:

> *And God raised us up with Christ and seated us with him in the heavenly realms in Christ Jesus, in order that in the coming ages he might show the incomparable riches of his grace, expressed in his kindness to us in Christ Jesus. (Ephesians 2:6-7)*

As Christ's representatives on this earth, we are ambassadors for his heavenly realm. Therefore, we have been equipped to carry out our assignment.

We speak and act according to his desire and purpose. We are clothed with distinguishing heavenly garments—robes of righteousness (Isaiah 61:10)—the national dress of God's kingdom. We share in diplomatic immunity, for Jesus said, *I have given you authority to trample on snakes and scorpions and to overcome all the power of the enemy; nothing will harm you.* (Luke 10:19)

How do we receive this authority and put it to use?

Jesus is the name that is above all names. It packs a powerful punch. We cannot exercise authority in the name of the President of the United States or in the name of a corporate CEO. No, it is only the anointed name of Jesus that carries supreme power:

Therefore God exalted him to the highest place and gave him the name that is above every name, that at the name of Jesus every knee should bow, in heaven and on earth and under the earth, and every tongue confess that Jesus Christ is Lord, to the glory of God the Father. (Philippians 2:9-11)

Just as an ambassador uses the name of their country when they sign documents and issue orders, we utilize the name of Jesus in our spiritual encounters. We are acting on his behalf. Therefore, we are endorsed by the Ruler of the Universe. And here is the good news! Jesus said he would act according to our prayers:

And I will do whatever you ask in my name, so that the Son may bring glory to the Father. You may ask me for anything in my name, and I will do it. (John 14:13-14)

So, we bring our petitions and prayers to God "in the

name of Jesus." We pray for healing "in the name of Jesus." We cast out demons "in the name of Jesus." Anything we ask or do for the Kingdom of God should be done "in the name of Jesus" because he has promised to answer that request.

How can we actually put that to work? How will the name of Jesus empower us to overcome the obstacles we face on a daily basis?

When my daughters were young, they had the typical struggles with fear. "Mom, I'm afraid. My bedroom is too dark. Can I turn on the light?" Or "I don't want to speak in front of my classmates. Can I stay home today?" Normal kid stuff and normal adult stuff too!

I taught my daughters to counter those fears by using their authority in Christ. They did not suppress the fear, cover their heads with a blanket, or pretend to be sick and stay home from school.

Just as Jesus used the word of God to defeat the enemy in the wilderness, my daughters and I used the word of God as a weapon. When fear would strike, we prayed like Jesus did when he confronted his enemy. We took scripture and personalized it by saying:

In the name of Jesus, fear, be gone! For God has not given me the spirit of fear; but of power, and of love, and of a sound mind. (2 Timothy 1:7, KJV)

Was it an immediate solution? Sometimes. We used the name of Jesus and the authority of scripture again and again until all fear had dissolved.

If I find myself battling doubt or unbelief, I command a spirit of doubt to be gone "in the name of Jesus." When I bless someone or ask God to act in their behalf, I always ask "in the name of Jesus." It is his name that contains the authority that we need for victory.

These are just a few examples of how the word of God and the name of Jesus triumphs over our daily struggles. There are countless promises in the Bible that we can use to bring change into a situation. His name empowers us to be victorious!

The Flow of Authority

In order to further understand the concept of authority in the Kingdom of God, we need to realize that it functions in specific ways. Like a physical body, every cell has a certain place and function.

There is a head, Jesus Christ, and we are all parts of the body joined together to uphold one another. A skeleton has a definite structure...the arm bones must be connected to the shoulder or else they cannot rotate and move according to God's plan. In the same way, we are fit together in harmony with God's original plan for the body:

Instead, speaking the truth in love, we will
in all things grow up into him who is the Head,
that is, Christ. From him the whole body, joined
and held together by every supporting ligament,
grows and builds itself up in love, as each
part does its work. (Ephesians 4:15-16)

We are not designed to function independently. As we mature, we also learn to be under spiritual authority.

To illustrate this concept, let's look at a story from scripture about a Roman centurion, a soldier who commanded one hundred men. This warrior of Rome demonstrated his understanding of authority when he approached Jesus with a request to heal his ailing servant:

The centurion replied, "Lord, I do not deserve
to have you come under my roof. But just say the
word, and my servant will be healed. For I myself
am a man under authority, with soldiers under me.
I tell this one, 'Go,' and he goes; and that one,
'Come,' and he comes. I say to my servant, 'Do
this,' and he does it." When Jesus heard this, he
was astonished and said to those following him,
"I tell you the truth, I have not found anyone in
Israel with such great faith. (Matthew 8:8-10)

The centurion understood the flow and function of authority from two dimensions. He commanded troops to do his bidding, but he was also positioned under someone else and subject to them. The Roman centurion grasped the importance of using his personal authority while at the same time being submitted to a higher authority. He understood that if Jesus spoke a few words into the spiritual realm, they would be followed.

Jesus called this "great faith." The centurion's understanding of the situation demonstrated that faith and authority are interconnected. They were the key to healing for his servant.

Each of us is called to walk in a measure of God's authority. Without a working knowledge and application of this concept, we will never fulfill our individual destiny and see his promises come to pass.

Here are five principles that are necessary to successfully activate our authority in Christ:

1. **Believe that he rules and reigns and has delegated that authority to us.** If we don't believe it, we will not exercise it. Like the police officers in the intersection who trust that the traffic will stop for them, we must also find the confidence to believe our faith-filled actions will get the desired results.

2. **Remain humble.** Our confidence is not in ourselves, but in Christ and the victory that he purchased for us. We can do nothing in

our own name, but everything in his!

3. **Develop a degree of boldness, courage, and faith to exercise authority**. Whether we are praying, addressing some spiritual concern, or helping others, the name of Jesus is our guarantee of victory.

4. **Rely on God for wisdom and direction.** The right has been delegated to us, but we must act in accordance with the prompting of the Holy Spirit. We are not acting independently, but are a living part of His body.

5. **Honor the authority over us.** That might be parents, teachers, police, pastors, or others. We move in authority to the degree that we honor and are submitted to those who are placed above us.

The backbone of the Christian life is knowing and using our authority. Temptations, evil influences, and our own weak nature challenge us on a daily basis. As we understand and exercise our spiritual authority, we overcome these obstacles and find victory in Christ's name.

Father,

*Help me to understand and walk in the
authority you have given me. Strengthen me
to be a good steward over the areas which are
mine to maintain. Teach me to use your name
Jesus whenever I pray and use your word as a
weapon to overcome any obstacles. May I see
results of your victory in my life. In Jesus name.*

Amen

Chapter 5

COMMUNITY...CONNECTING FOR GROWTH

The Kingdom of God is not confined to a physical building. It is alive and moving, growing and expanding under the direction of God. It lives and breathes just like any living organism. The Church, God's assembly of believers across the globe, is comprised of people.

God's majestic plan for His family is much more than four walls, pews, a few classrooms, and offices. God planned for a community, a global family that is united and connected to him.

He called this association the "Body of Christ," a term used to express the relationship we share. Jesus is the head of the body. We are a community of believers who are interrelated, cohesive, and linked to each other and to God who has renewed our lives.

Just like a physical body has many parts and each has its function, so the Body of Christ is comprised of many different parts. Each one is alive, active, and flowing with the energy and life of God. Individually, we are one piece of that life and one piece in the function of the body:

In this way we are like the various parts of a human body. Each part gets its meaning from the body as a whole, not the other way around. The body we're talking about is Christ's body of chosen people. Each of us finds our meaning and function as a part of his body...let's just go ahead and be what we were made to be, without enviously or pridefully comparing ourselves with each other, or trying to be something we aren't. (Romans 12:4-5, The Message Bible)

The Apostle Paul wrote this about the body of Christ: *Now you are the body of Christ, and each one of you is a part of it.* (1 Corinthians 12:27) We may belong to different denominations, but we are one in him. Each of us expresses a different part of the complex nature of Christ.

For example, one denomination might focus on the serving nature of Christ and so they represent the "hands" of the body. Another group may be more visionary and so represent the "eyes" of the body. And still another church assembly may stress the importance of compassion and minister through the "heart" of God. Each is strictly an expression of a particular appendage of the body. We need every part to function as a whole!

We are a "body," connected and related, and we are also a family. We relate to God Himself...Father, Son, and Spirit. We also relate to each other as living pieces of his greater work. When it comes to maintaining a healthy spiritual environment, both aspects of community are important. They provide a deeper understanding into community life in the Family of God.

Connecting Upward to God

My children and I spent hours together laughing, baking cookies, playing games, and chatting about life in general. Now, I pick up the phone, but it is much more satisfying when we meet in person. I wrap my arms around them and demonstrate my love. Open hearts and open arms! The one-on-one personal touch from a mom never grows old.

Where did the parent and child relationship begin?

The special bond began in the Garden of Eden. Mankind walked and talked with their heavenly parent on a daily basis.

Did Adam approach God with a list of things he needed done? Would Eve plead with God for divine intervention? Did their times together include tears, anguish, and desperate cries?

I don't think so. They were not forced to ask for the essentials of life. The male and female were in perfect harmony. They enjoyed a dynamic relationship with pure and undamaged emotions. Every need was met and Adam and Eve walked in perfect health. They approached God only to talk.

And God answered.

Imagine for a moment what their conversation could have been. Maybe God asked, "How was your day today, Adam?" Or, "Have you tried the fruit from that tree yet, Eve…it's delicious. I made it just for you!" It was probably a simple conversation between the Creator and his creation, a friendship between the divine and mankind.

Have you ever called a friend on the phone just to chat? When two people care about each other, they strengthen that bond through conversations. That is the way God wants to relate to you. He did it with the male and female in the garden and he desires the same relationship with you today.

Adam and Eve received life from God during their encounters. Each day God breathed His words and nature into the male and female. I don't think it was a stiff, "Hello, Sir. Nice to see you again" from Adam. I want to think the male and female ran with joy every time they saw God enter the garden. They ran unabashed to their Father and were swept up into his adoring arms.

Love brought God into the garden...love for his Creation. And love drew both God and mankind together, day after day, month after month, even year after year. They never grew tired of each other. Each day was fresh with the life and learning only God had to give.

Perhaps one day they spoke about the stars. Another day the conversation centered upon the fish in the sea. The next meeting brought a lively exchange over the merits of animal life within the garden. Any and every question Adam or Eve had, God could and would answer. He had given them an insatiable desire for knowledge, but the answers came from him alone as they talked about the universe and its many facets.

Then the day came when Adam and Eve didn't come running.

Instead, they hid from God. The shame of their disobedience overpowered the joy of the friendship. What a drastic change! God had given them everything. He loved them passionately. But now they hid in fear of Him? It must have broken his heart to see the failure of their relationship. Something so perfect was destroyed so completely.

Fortunately for us, God provided a way for that human-God relationship to be restored. Through Jesus we can know the surety of his divine love once again.

Can we experience the same vibrancy of relationship with God that Adam and Eve enjoyed?

Yes, definitely!

The same God, who met them in the Garden of Eden desires, even yearns for times of fellowship with us.

Communing with God is giving Him access to our heart. We share who we are with our Creator, and he responds with an overwhelming sense of his presence. Even when we sin, make a mistake, or fall short of God's best for our life, we can maintain a place of fellowship with God. He does not demand perfection, only a willing and repentant heart:

But if we walk in the light, as he is in the light, we have fellowship with one another, and the blood of Jesus, his Son, purifies us from all sin. If we claim to be without sin, we deceive ourselves and the truth is not in us. If we confess our sins, he is faithful and just and will forgive us our sins and purify us from all unrighteousness. (1 John 1:7-9)

Each of us has a garden in our soul. It belongs to God

alone. Jesus said, *If anyone loves me, he will obey my teaching. My Father will love him, and we will come to him and make our home with him.* (John 14:23)

Our inner garden begs for the touch and presence of God. God longs to enter and walk through the intimate areas of our being…to converse, repair, and restore our garden to its original state.

He hopes to relate to us on a daily basis and infuse us with his life. It may be in quiet times sitting and just talking to him. Other times it might be reading the Bible for insight into our world. It's a never-ending love story of God and man communicating with one another. We call it prayer.

The Lord's Prayer: Communing with God

How do you begin communicating with an eternal, all-knowing God? The disciples of Jesus had a similar question for their Master. They asked Jesus, *Lord, teach us to pray.* (Luke 11:1)

The twelve disciples were familiar with prayer, in fact, they had all kinds of rules and regulations for how to approach God. Jews had specific days for fasting, designated days of holy prayer, and even sacrifices that assured them they were heard by God. But the disciples understood Jesus offered something different…a new way of relating to God and a revolutionary path in prayer.

Jesus didn't respond by giving them one single prayer to repeat over and over again. Instead of what to say, he showed them how to pray. You may recognize it as "The Lord's Prayer:"

> *Our Father in heaven, Hallowed be Your name. Your kingdom come. Your will be done on earth as it is in heaven. Give us this day our daily bread. And forgive us our debts, as we forgive our debtors. And do not lead us into temptation, but deliver us from the evil one. For Yours is the kingdom and the power and the glory forever. Amen. (Matthew 6:9-13, NKJV)*

By following the example Jesus gave His disciples, we can commune with God in a similar fashion. Repeating these same words is a start; however, if we want to expand our relationship with God in prayer, we recognize that the Lord 's Prayer is a pattern. Instead of repeating it by rote, we begin by examining the underlying themes to the prayer:

> ***Our Father in heaven, Hallowed be Your name.*** Jesus showed his disciples that they could approach their Heavenly Father without acts of sacrifice or good works. They didn't need to earn a place of recognition. As they acknowledged His supremacy over their

life, they could begin by worshiping him. (Psalm 84, Psalm 100, Psalm 145)

Your kingdom come. Your will be done on earth as it is in heaven. God has a will that he wants to be accomplished on earth, both in your individual life and throughout the entire world. You can pray for God's universal will to be completed...petitions for peace, an outpouring of God's goodness, or the sharing of the gospel throughout the world. You can also focus on the specifics of his will for your life and others. Pray that it would be known and realized. (John 4:34, John 5:30)

Give us this day our daily bread. Jesus wanted his disciples to rest in God's provision. Ask and depend on God to provide your daily necessities. He has a vast storehouse full of the requirements for life. God is able to provide whatever you need. (Psalm 103:5, Psalm 111:5)

And forgive us our debts, as we forgive our debtors. The characteristic that distinguishes Christianity from other religions is forgiveness. God removes the stigma of our mistakes, but then he asks us to extend that same grace to others. He tells us to release the offense and the offender into his hands. Not always easy, but always necessary. (Matthew 18:21-35, Ephesians 4:32, 1 Peter 3:9)

And do not lead us into temptation, but deliver us from the evil one. We have an enemy, an adversary who is evil and bent on destruction. Ask God to guide you on the path that leads away from temptation and evil. (Hebrews 2:18, 1 Corinthians 10:13)

For Yours is the kingdom and the power and the glory forever. Amen. Finally, worship the Lord again. Think of the goodness of God and how he has been faithful to you. He is worthy of your praise and thanksgiving. (Psalm 19:1, Psalm 57:5, Psalm 138)

Does it matter what words you use? Is there a certain position that is required…sitting, standing, kneeling? What about the time of day or the place?

The ideal prayer does not exist, only an honest heart that wants to know God. Remember, it is a conversation with God. God is interested in you, not perfection in prayer. Just talk to Him whenever and wherever you like. Then stop and listen. He will want to respond to you.

Yes! God will talk back to you.

Sometimes in a still, small voice in your inner man. Sometimes He will answer through the Bible as you read it. Often, God will direct your path and circumstances so that His will is done. Entire books have been written on how God speaks to us today, so this is just a small sample of how and why God will answer. Realize prayer is a two-way street and you should expect Him to respond.

God desires communion with humanity. From the first book of Genesis to the end of the Bible, God is intimately interacts with people. The final book in the Bible speaks of heaven and God's final plan to dwell permanently with mankind. He is looking forward to an eternity in our presence. And we will be with Him:

> *And I heard a loud voice from the throne saying, "Now the dwelling of God is with men, and he will live with them. They will be his people, and God himself will be with them and be their God. (Revelation 21:3)*

Adam received life from his relationship with God. The breath of God created him and continued fellowship sustained him.

God is the source for our life as well. What Adam and Eve had in the garden is still available. Take the time to experience this vital, vibrant experience with God yourself. He welcomes you with open arms.

The Family of God

The vascular system of a plant consists of two conduits called the "phloem" and "xylem." They conduct the nutrients and water up and down the plant stalk, similar to the blood vessels in an animal. One brings the essentials up the shaft; the other brings them down. Without the phloem and xylem a plant would starve from lack of nutrition and the essential building blocks needed to grow.

Much like a plant, humans also require some basic nutrients to grow and sustain life. We need a flow of kindness and compassion from others directed towards us. And we must have an outward flow of God's love targeting those around us. Give and take. Without human companionship and care, we too would perish.

From the first, God ordained that man should be in community with others. *"It is not good that the man should be alone."*(Genesis 2:18) He created woman and they worked side-by-side in the garden tending the handiwork of God. They were the ideal co-laborers with one another...one mind, one heart, one purpose. Life was a joyful experience as they worked together to fulfill God's plan.

Years later, God chose a man named Abraham to begin another extraordinary unit, a covenant family. He selected Abraham because he understood the importance of family and would teach his children the ways of the Lord:

> *Abraham will surely become a great and powerful nation, and all nations on earth will be blessed through him. For I have chosen him, so that he will direct his children and his household after him to keep the way of the Lord by doing what is right and just, so that the Lord will bring about for Abraham what he has promised him." (Genesis 18:18-19)*

Abraham had a son named Isaac. Isaac had a son named Jacob. Jacob, whose name was changed to Israel, had twelve sons. They became the twelve tribes of Israel and the covenant family of God was formed. Five hundred years later, Moses led these people out of Egypt and into Canaan, a land promised to the spiritual family of God. They became the nation of Israel.

The idea of a covenant spiritual family would expand to include anyone who accepted Jesus as the Son of God. Through Christ we are adopted into the family of God and become His sons and daughters:....*he predestined us to be adopted as his sons through Jesus Christ, in accordance with his pleasure and will.* (Ephesians 1:5)

You were never created to be alone or to live your life in isolation. God's promise to you is that He will be... *A father to the fatherless, a defender of widows, is God in his holy dwelling. God sets the lonely in families...*(Psalm 68:5-6)

When I first moved to Georgia, I lived six hundred miles away from my natural family. With two small children in tow, I did not have the time to join clubs or casually socialize in search of new relationships. God provided friends and a spiritual family through my neighbors, Sandy and Pat. They became my sisters in the Lord. Although we now live on opposite sides of the United States, we are still close, lifelong friends.

During this time, I also needed a mother figure to mentor me in practical ways. The Lord brought Lois into my life and she immediately took me under her wing. Lois taught me a variety of skills from how to set a banquet table to counseling someone in need. We baked casseroles, taught young girls, shared personal challenges and triumphs, and laughed and rejoiced as women who loved the Lord. Lois modeled femininity to me as she encouraged me to mature as a woman.

A spiritual family is much like a natural family. There are highs and lows, good times and bad, blessings and challenges to overcome. Through it all, God has stressed the importance of joint co-operation as we all endeavor to mature in Christ-likeness.

The Bible states again and again that we are to

respond to one another with the love of God. Those words "one another" are significant. They indicate a symbiotic relationship, a mutually beneficial coexistence, between members of God's family. Here are a few of the "one another" principles that God has chosen to emphasize to His family:

Love one another. *A new command I give you: Love one another. As I have loved you, so you must love one another. By this all men will know that you are my disciples, if you love one another.* (John 13:34)

Accept one another. *Accept one another, then, just as Christ accepted you, in order to bring praise to God.* (Romans 15:7)

Care for one another. *Be completely humble and gentle; be patient, bearing with one another in love.* (Ephesians 4:2)

Honor one another. *Be devoted to one another in brotherly love. Honor one another above yourselves.* (Romans 12:10)

Encourage one another. *Therefore encourage one another and build each other up, just as in fact you are doing.* (1 Thessalonians 5:11)

Forgive one another. *Be kind and compassionate to one another, forgiving each other, just as in Christ God forgave you.* (Ephesians 4:32)

Instruct one another. *I myself am convinced, my brothers, that you yourselves are full of goodness, complete in knowledge and competent to instruct one another.* (Romans 15:14)

Serve one another.*....serve one another in love.* (Galatians 5:13)

There is a synergy when God's people come together, a spiritual dynamic that is infused with his power. As we live together in unity, God is able to pour out his blessing upon us:

How good and pleasant it is when brothers live together in unity! It is like precious oil poured on the head, running down on the beard, running down on Aaron's beard, down upon the collar of his robes. It is as if the dew of Hermon were falling on Mount Zion. For there the Lord bestows his blessing, even life forevermore. (Psalm 133)

We connect to God and we connect to people. Communing with Him and continuing in fellowship with his people have always been a part of God's plan.

Both are a source of life to the growing Christian. Both contain the necessary elements required for wholesome, balanced living.

You are never alone. He has promised never to leave us or forsake us.

Father,

Thank You for relationships and the ability to talk to you whenever and wherever I choose. I desire to know You more, so please help me in this. Show me how You communicate and make me sensitive to Your voice and ways. Place me in a group of believers who know and love You so that I may learn more and grow. Thank you, Lord, for loving me.

Amen

Chapter 6

SUFFICIENCY...THE GOD WHO IS MORE THAN ENOUGH

God reveals himself in unique ways. Often we glimpse a facet of his divine nature in the midst of challenging circumstances. My husband and I have experienced him as the one who returns what has been stolen, a restorer of wealth, and a rebuilder of dreams. The following is a personal example of his faithfulness to my family.

Following my mother's death, our family struggled to find an equitable way to divide her estate. Part of my inheritance included a rare antique music box. During the settling of the estate, a family member sold it in an unauthorized, under-the-table deal and confiscated the money.

I could have taken legal action, but I released the situation into God's hands. The next day a friend of the family was browsing in a local antique store. He recognized the music box hidden under a blanket and we recovered the item. God restored my inheritance in a miraculous way!

A few years later, we experienced the lowest point in our married life. It began with a corporate move to St. Louis. In less than a year, I was uprooted from my home, family, and friends of twenty years and plunged into a swirl of uncontrollable change.

Empty-nest syndrome arrived; my daughters now lived ten hours away. The corporate promotion promised to my husband turned into a layoff after nine months. We were forced to sell our new custom-built home. I had to walk away from a promising position with a world-wide ministry, as we relocated once again. Paul and I moved six times in the next three years. I was confused, lonely, and grieving our losses.

In spite of the layoff, I kept encouraging Paul that God would not demote him, but provide a livelihood that was equal or better than the previous one. Finally, we relocated to Massachusetts and began to rebuild our shattered lives.

We spent the first year in a cramped apartment

waiting for our house in St. Louis to be sold. The second year we lived in a rental home infested with mice...it was a constant battle! But two years later, we were able to purchase a lovely home similar to the one we had lost in St. Louis. My husband had a new job and was making even more money than before! That's restoration.

The story of God's ability to restore and rebuild doesn't end there. Three years later, the gasket failed on our upstairs toilet. For one full day, water cascaded down two flights of stairs, drenching the main floor, and pooling in the basement. I received the emergency call from our cat-sitter while on vacation.

My first reaction might sound peculiar...I began to laugh. Believing that our rebuilt home would be even superior to the previous one, I remembered a scripture from the book of Haggai:

'The glory of this present house will be greater than the glory of the former house,' says the Lord Almighty. 'And in this place I will grant peace,' declares the Lord Almighty." Haggai 2:9

It took six weeks to gut and rebuild over one third of the house. But, we were able to replace the wooden floors with a superior grade of flooring, improve the quality of carpet by several upgrades, and receive an allocation of money to purchase new furniture for the kitchen and dining room. The entire house was repainted and refurbished. Our renovated residence not only looked brand new, it was decorated with more expensive furnishings.

We experienced God as *Jehovah Shuv*, a name I have coined. He is the God who restores. And when he restores, it is even bigger and better than before!

The All-Sufficient God

Four thousand years ago, a righteous man named Abraham lacked an heir to carry on his family name. He was seventy-five years old and his aging wife Sarah was well past her child-bearing years. The situation appeared rather hopeless in the natural scheme of things, but Abraham had received a promise from God.

Abraham would have a son. All nations would be blessed through that son. His descendants would be as plentiful as the stars in the sky. His offspring would dwell in the land as far as Abraham's eyes could see.

Big promises from a big God!

But twenty-five years later, the promise remained unfulfilled. Abraham was probably wondering, "How is this all going to take place? I am not getting any younger, and neither is my wife, Sarah."

The Bible tells us that Abraham knew he could trust

God to stand behind his promises. Even though the situation appeared impossible, Abraham chose to believe that God could and would fulfill that promise.

What amazing faith in God! Abraham realized that somehow God would provide him with a son to fulfill the pledge. In response to Abraham's simple and unshakable trust, God appeared and revealed himself as the Almighty One who was well able to perform everything he had promised:

When Abram was ninety-nine years old, the Lord appeared to him and said, "I am God Almighty; walk before me and be blameless. I will confirm my covenant between me and you and will greatly increase your numbers." Genesis 17:1

The Hebrew word used for "Almighty" is *El Shaddai*, the all sufficient one. God was saying to Abraham "I am able to do anything. I am more than sufficient for everything you need."

Abraham's part was to simply believe and rely on God's faithfulness and power. God would do the rest!

Have you ever had a pressing need and wondered, "How will I ever find a solution to this problem?

All of us experience those situations that are beyond our human means and understanding. So, where do we seek our answers? Who can we trust to be reliable? And how will our needs be met? Just as

Abraham met the God who was "all sufficient," we can experience the nature of God as the one who is more than enough.

God is the Provider

When God created the Garden of Eden, He wasn't working on a budget! He had no limits. God spoke the best into being and created the epitome of an environment that would provide, entertain, and shelter his creations. Food was plentiful and diverse. The sights, smells, and sounds must have soothed and stimulated God's creation with sheer perfection.

What did Adam and Eve lack?

Absolutely nothing. They lived in a perfect climate in a perfect state of innocence. Every need was met.

Has God changed? Is He still concerned with our needs and able to provide on a daily basis?

Yes! The same God who spoke with Adam and provided for his every need has not evolved into another being. He is the immutable and unchangeable one who *is the same yesterday, today, and forever.* (Hebrews 13:8)

God's character never wavers. We can rely on the fact that he is steadfast and true. He not only meets our needs, but surpasses them:

God can do anything, you know—far more than

you could ever imagine or guess or request in your wildest dreams! He does it not by pushing us around but by working within us, his Spirit deeply and gently within us. (Ephesians 3:20-21, The Message Bible)

When meeting someone for the first time, I introduce myself with "Hi, my name is Pam." When the question "And what do you do?" is asked, I could respond in a variety of ways.

I could answer with "I'm a pastor." Or "I am the guest speaker." I may be "Lisa and Laurie's mother," a common response as they were growing up. I might also be "Paul's wife" if we are in a business setting relating to his work. What is it that they need to know about me in this particular arena?

God responds to us in a similar manner. In our encounters with God, he is quick to express his nature in that particular time. He doesn't need to be the healer, if healing is not required. God doesn't need to be the victorious one when battles are not fought.

God shows up as who we need at the specific time when we need Him.

This is how we get to know Him! Like a diamond that shines brilliantly as light reflects off of its many angles, God is multi-faceted and infinitely diverse.

How you experience him in this life is only a fraction

of the complete nature of God. In both the Old and New Testaments, the people of God experienced him in various ways. As each need arose, they had the privilege of knowing their God in a novel way.

When God chose to reveal himself, they responded by describing him with a new name. As we observe how our Biblical ancestors related to God in their specific need, we can also take heart that he will do the same for us.

The Names of God

The first unique name for God in the Bible is *El Shaddai*, the all sufficient one. (Genesis 17:1) Abraham experienced God's power to revive his and Sarah's aging bodies and bring forth a child. God was sufficient even in the midst of their barrenness and a son was born to Abraham and Sarah.

Abraham also knew God as *Jehovah Jireh*, the God who would provide. As a test, God asked Abraham to take his son Isaac on Mount Moriah and offer him as a sacrifice. In the midst of a difficult situation, Abraham obeyed. He trusted that the one who had given him a son would not ultimately destroy him.

Abraham passed the test with glorious results. God provided a ram caught in a thicket. In that place on Mount Moriah, Abraham experienced God as the one who would provide for him:

So Abraham called that place The Lord Will Provide. And to this day it is said, "On the mountain of the Lord it will be provided." (Genesis 22:14)

Five hundred years later, a man named Moses stood on another mountain. He climbed it to see a wondrous sight...a fiery bush that did not burn! It was here, on Mount Horeb, that God appeared to Moses and called him to deliver the nation of Israel from the oppression of the Egyptians. Moses suffered with a bout of insecurity and needed the reassurance that he would not be alone in the task laid before him:

Moses said to God, "Suppose I go to the Israelites and say to them, 'The God of your fathers has sent me to you,' and they ask me, 'What is his name?' Then what shall I tell them?"

God said to Moses, "I AM WHO I AM.(or I will be what I will be) This is what you are to say to the Israelites: 'I AM has sent me to you.'"

God also said to Moses, "Say to the Israelites, 'The Lord, the God of your fathers—the God of Abraham, the God of Isaac and the God of Jacob—has sent me to you.' This is my name forever, the name by which I am to be remembered from generation to generation. (Exodus 3:13-15)

Does God know how to issue a calling card, or what?

"Hi, Moses. Let me introduce myself to you. Your fathers knew me as *El Shaddai,* but I want you to know me as *I AM.*"Tell the people *I AM* has sent you."(The Hebrew word for *I AM* is *YHWH* which we pronounce *Jehovah.*)

God's name is like a blank check waiting to filled in

I AM _____!

Moses relied on supernatural signs and wonders to persuade Pharaoh to release Israel from bondage. *I AM* was there at every confrontation. Moses needed water and food in the desert for the millions of followers. *I AM* provided water from a rock and manna that rained down every morning from heaven.

When the water was bitter and undrinkable at Marah, *I AM* showed Moses a piece of wood which could be cast into the waters to make them sweet. I AM became *Jehovah Rapha* to the Israelites, the God who heals:

> *He said, "If you listen carefully to the voice of the Lord your God and do what is right in his eyes, if you pay attention to his commands and keep all his decrees, I will not bring on you any of the diseases I brought on the Egyptians, for **I am the Lord, who heals you.**" (Exodus 15:26)*

In a battle with the fierce Amalekites, *I AM* became *Jehovah Nissi*, the God who is a banner of victory.

Two men, Aaron and Hur, raised Moses' hands to heaven during the ensuing battle. As long as his hands were raised, the Israelites prevailed. God became their sign of victory:

> *Moses built an altar and called it **The Lord is my Banner.** He said, "For hands were lifted up to the throne of the Lord. (Exodus 17:15)*

Hundreds of years later, Gideon knew *I AM* as *Jehovah Shalom*, the God of peace. He received a divine call to lead Israel against their Midianite oppressors. Afraid of dying because he had come face to face with an angel of the Lord, Gideon was comforted by God's peace:

> *So Gideon built an altar to the Lord there and called it **The Lord is Peace.** Judges 6:24*

To David, the shepherd boy who became a king, *I AM* was the ultimate shepherd! With his vast knowledge of herding sheep, David understood the greater truth of how Jehovah could relate to him as a shepherd. David's association with God still stands as an example for us to follow thousands of years later. David called him *Jehovah Raah*, the God who is my shepherd:

> *The LORD is my shepherd, I lack nothing. He makes me lie down in green pastures, he leads me beside quiet waters, he refreshes my soul. He*

guides me along the right paths for his name's sake. Even though I walk through the darkest valley, I will fear no evil, for you are with me; your rod and your staff, they comfort me. You prepare a table before me in the presence of my enemies. You anoint my head with oil; my cup overflows. Surely your goodness and love will follow me all the days of my life, and I will dwell in the house of the LORD forever. (Psalm 23)

The Prophet Jeremiah foresaw a day when *I AM* would shower his righteousness upon the nation of Israel. A king would come and establish a righteous rule on the throne of David. Humanity would experience God as *Jehovah Tsidekenu*, the God of righteousness:

*"The days are coming," declares the Lord, "when I will raise up to David a righteous Branch, a King who will reign wisely and do what is just and right in the land. In his days Judah will be saved and Israel will live in safety. This is the name by which he will be called: **The Lord Our Righteousness.** (Jeremiah 23:5-6)*

The Prophet Ezekiel had a vision of a holy city Jerusalem and the overwhelming sense of God's presence in the midst. *I AM* became *Jehovah Shammah*, the God whose presence is there. He wrote:

*"And the name of the city from that time on will be: **The Lord is there.**" (Ezekiel 48:35)*

The All-sufficient. Provider. I AM. Healer. Banner of Victory. Peace. Shepherd. Righteousness. The One who is there. As exciting as these names are, they are only a small glimpse of the infinite person of God. We shouldn't limit Jehovah to these few names. God is much more complex than that.

In the New Testament, Jesus is known by many names. He was the "Bread of Life" when he fed the multitudes. He was the "Gate" when he declared Himself to be the true path to eternal life. Jesus was "The Lamb of God" when he became the Passover sacrifice for sin to the nation of Israel. Jesus was known to the people as "The Resurrection and the Life" when he demonstrated his authority over death by raising Lazarus from the dead.

There are hundreds of names for God throughout the Bible and each one reflects only one aspect of his infinite character. As you encounter the divine nature of God in your everyday life, you, too, will discover he is all sufficient for your every need.

The God of Promise

Do you lack insight in a situation? Are you wrestling with a decision that must be made? The God of all wisdom and understanding has the answers. God deals with the tangible and material things in life, but also the intangible:

If any of you lacks wisdom, he should ask God, who gives generously to all without finding fault, and it will be given to him. (James 1:5)

The Apostle Paul wrote of God's provision to the churches in Philippi and Corinth. He assured them God would intervene in their behalf. Paul had been beaten, imprisoned, persecuted, shipwrecked, and threatened, but he had learned one crucial underlying truth. Jehovah had never abandoned him. He was always a source of supply for Paul:

And my God will meet all your needs according to his glorious riches in Christ Jesus. (Philippians 4:19)

...And God is able to make all grace abound to you, so that in all things at all times, having all that you need, you will abound in every good work. (2 Corinthians 9:6-9)

These scripture verses describe the sufficiency of God...all things at all times, so that you will have all that you need. That's God's blank check to you.

What do you need to fulfill your destiny with God?

How will you fill in your blank check?

The Bible is filled with hundreds of promises that apply to every person. Healing. Finances. Peace. Wholeness. The list is endless. The word of God is alive and has the power to change us and those things that concern us.

The following guidelines will help you to see the promises of God come to pass.

1. ***Define your need.*** If you have a Bible, look up scriptures containing the key words that pertain to it. For example, if you need strength, look up scriptures that speak of God giving you strength. Philippians 4:13 is a good example: *I can do everything through him who gives me strength.*

Another tool to help you find God's truth for a specific situation is a "promise book." These are small books that have taken various scriptures, categorized them according to topic, and are easy to use. They are perfect for a new believer!

2. ***Believe.*** Once you have found God's perspective about your circumstances, believe that He wants to bring change. Begin to pray about your situation. Ask God if there is anything you must do to see the word of God become a reality in your life. We have

a part to play in the process of seeing God's provision manifest in our life.

Is there a condition to your promise?

You may find a scripture that states "if you…., then I (God) will…"As you begin to pray, trust that he is a God who loves you and only wants what is best for your life.

3. ***Do your part.*** Sometimes God may ask us to forgive those who have offended us. If you are asking for strength, God may impress upon you to sleep more hours or eat a healthier and balanced diet. He can be very practical! If you do your part, rest assured, he will do his!

4. ***Personalize the scripture.*** Put your name in the scripture passage. Using Philippians 4:13 as an example, I would say...

"Pam (or your name) can do everything through him who gives me strength."

By placing your name in the scripture text, you identify with it on a deeper level. The truth of the text begins to take root. Essentially, you are taking the living, God-breathed words of the Lord and planting them within. As they take root and grow, you will witness a change on the inside as well as in your outside circumstances. This is what the author James stated:

> *Submit to God and accept the word*
> *that he plants in your hearts, which is*
> *able to save you. (James 1:21)*

Jehovah is sufficient in all situations at all times. He is a never-ending reservoir of truth, wisdom, and power to change even the most difficult of circumstances. Trust Him. You will never be disappointed!

Lord,

Because You are the source of all things, I come humbly to you today with my needs. I believe that You alone are the solution to any problem or circumstance that I face.

Father, please give me wisdom.

Father, please give me strength as I face the challenges of life.

I choose to trust You and have faith that You will meet my every need. Thank you, Lord for your provision in my life.

Amen

The Promises of God

Abundant Life....John 10:10

A Crown of Life...Revelation 2:10

A Heavenly Home...John 14:1-3

A New Name...Isaiah 62:1-2

Answers to Prayer...1 John 5:14

Assurance...2 Timothy 1:12

Confidence...Philippians 4:13

Comfort...Isaiah 51:3

Companionship....John 15:15

Deliverance...2 Timothy 4:18

Fellowship with Jesus...Matthew 18:19

Fruitfulness....John 15:4-5

Gifts of the Spirit...1 Corinthians 12

God's Protection...Psalm 18:2

Guidance...Proverbs 3:5-6

Healing...Psalm 103:3; 147:3

Hope...Hebrews 6:18-19

Joy...Isaiah 35:10

Knowledge...Jeremiah 24:7

Liberty...Romans 8:2

Patience...James 1:3-4; Isaiah 40:31

Peace...John 14:27

Power...John 14:12

Renewal...Titus 3:5

Rest...Hebrews 4:9-11

Restoration...Isaiah 57:18; 1John 1:9

Rich Rewards...Matthew 10:42

Spiritual fullness...John 6:35

Victory...1 John 5:4

Wisdom...James 1:5

Chapter 7
GROWING IN GRACE

Every year I plant seeds in my garden hoping for an abundant harvest. Like all optimistic backyard-farmers, I expect to reap a reward for my months of effort.

Growing vigorous, fruitful plants is hard work. Soil composition is critical to their health and development. Fertilizer is necessary, as well as constant watering and weeding. However, the satisfaction I receive from watching my plants grow and tasting the fruits of my labor is unsurpassed.

Each species matures according to its specific timetable, and the wait stretches my patience. I am delighted when I finally bite into a juicy, red tomato.

The growing process delights me. And our growth delights God.

Sowing the Seed

Natural plants need a healthy environment to grow. So do we.

Jesus taught about our spiritual lives being like a plant. He warned believers of the negatives forces that could work against us and limit the growth.

Christ compared our spiritual life to seed that is sown on various types of ground. Some of the seeds grew and came to maturity, but many did not. To illustrate this principle, Jesus taught his disciples the parable of the farmer and the seed:

"Listen! A farmer went out to sow his seed. As he was scattering the seed, some fell along the path, and the birds came and ate it up. Some fell on rocky places, where it did not have much soil. It sprang up quickly, because the soil was shallow. But when the sun came up, the plants were scorched, and they withered because they had no root. Other seed fell among thorns, which grew up and choked the plants, so that they did not bear grain. Still other seed fell on good soil. It came up, grew and produced a crop, some multiplying thirty, some sixty, some a hundred times…"

The farmer sows the word. Some people are like seed along the path, where the word is sown. As soon as they hear it, Satan comes and takes away the word that was sown in them. Others, like seed sown on rocky places, hear the word and at once receive it with joy. But since they have no root, they last only a short time. When trouble or persecution comes because of the word, they quickly fall away. Still others, like seed sown among thorns, hear the word; but the worries of this life, the deceitfulness of wealth and the desires for other things come in and choke the word, making it unfruitful. Others, like seed sown on good soil, hear the word, accept it, and produce a crop—some thirty, some sixty, some a hundred times what was sown." (Mark 5:3-8, 13-20)

WE are the planting of the Lord! Whenever we read or hear God's word, it is like the seed in the parable. We can choose to receive his truth, allow it to take root, and then produce an abundant harvest. Or we can reject it like the rocky ground or permit outside influences to distract us. This limits the potential of God's word.

According to this parable, we should recognize certain elements will inhibit our spiritual growth. In order to mature and fulfill our destiny, we must avoid certain things: unbelief, troubles, worry, lure of wealth, and the lust for material goods. Don't allow them to uproot and choke off God's planting!

Pulling Spiritual Weeds

Weeding is a never-ending task in a garden. Those pesky weeds compete for space, choke out the other plantings, and rob the garden of its nutrients. How can a plant develop to maturity when constantly contending for its life?

Our spiritual life also has weeds that compete for time and energy. What kind of weeds are these?

False beliefs. Half-truths. Philosophies that have a basis in man's thoughts, not God's truth.

It's not enough to hear the truth. It is not even enough to believe the truth. We must take an active stance to expose the spiritual weeds and uproot them!

Our modern world offers a smorgasbord of spiritual experiences. There are religious doctrines and practices that appeal to every human whim. Combine that with belief systems that promote partial truths, and it becomes confusing.

How do we differentiate the truth from bogus beliefs?

If we limit our understanding of Christianity to a rational, mental appraisal, then we are merely comparing one philosophy with another. Mental ascent is not what defines our life as Christ's followers.

Christianity is not just a belief system, but a

relationship with a living, eternal God.

Access to this relationship comes through faith in his son, Jesus Christ. What distinguishes Christianity from the other religions of the world? Let us examine some exclusive characteristics of the Christian faith and identify any weeds that may be growing.

Jesus is God's Only Son. Some religions recognize several gods as worthy of worship. Others believe there are multiple sons of their god. Or, like ancient mythology, male and female gods may produce children that are divine. Many even believe that you can achieve the status of godhood through works.

According to the Bible, there is only one Son. He is, was, and will always be a divine and a genuine representation of his Father. His name is Jesus Christ and he stands alone as the only son of God:

> *The Word became flesh and made his dwelling*
> *among us. We have seen his glory, the glory*
> *of the One and Only, came from the Father,*
> *full of grace and truth. (John 1:14)*

Jesus is the One Way to the Father. People claim there are many ways to find God. One philosophy works as well as another. Some suggest meditative states as the path to inner awareness. Others point to a strict code of ethics as the way of advancement and favor.

Although there are many paths to religious expression, there is only one path to the true and living God. Jesus said *"I am the way, the truth, and the life. No one comes to the Father except through me."* (John 14:6)

Do not be fooled into accepting a counterfeit religious experience for the reality of a relationship with God. It may look, smell, and even taste good, but is it the genuine article? Are you experiencing the new life Jesus died to give you? Has your current path led you to a satisfying, life-giving association with a God who loves you?

Jesus is a Servant God. Many religions have gods that demand service from their worshipers. They require oblations, rituals, a strict code of behavior, some outward sign, or even human sacrifice to prove allegiance. Men and women serve the wishes of this demanding god.

However, when Jesus appeared on the earth, He came as a servant to humanity. His purpose was centered on what He could do for them. Christ's earthly mission was threefold:

> 1. He came to show us the exact nature of God. Jesus put aside his heavenly status and became a human. The world witnessed a perfect replica of the heavenly Father as Jesus modeled it to them.

2. Jesus shouldered the sin and disobedience of his creation. In their behalf, he was willing to pay the price and purchase redemption for mankind. Jesus became the sacrifice.

3. He continues to serve humanity by interceding in prayer for his people. Christ did not come to be served, although he could have commanded it. Rather he came to show us the dignity and humility of a being a servant:

Christ Jesus...being in very nature God, did not consider equality with God something to be grasped, but made himself nothing, taking the very nature of a servant, being made in human likeness. And being found in appearance as a man, he humbled himself and became obedient to death— even death on a cross! Therefore God exalted him to the highest place and gave him the name that is above every name, that at the name of Jesus every knee should bow, in heaven and on earth and under the earth, and every tongue confess that Jesus Christ is Lord, to the glory of God the Father. (Philippians 2:5-11)

Jesus Died for the Sins of All Humanity. Sin is nothing more than an act that displeases or offends God. That covers a very broad spectrum of acts, words, and thoughts most of which we would like to forget! Whatever our shortcomings, Jesus wiped the slate clean when He died on the cross:

> *Since we've compiled this long and sorry record*
> *as sinners (both us and them) and proved that*
> *we are utterly incapable of living the glorious*
> *lives God wills for us, God did it for us. Out of*
> *sheer generosity he put us in right standing with*
> *himself. A pure gift. He got us out of the mess*
> *we're in and restored us to where he always*
> *wanted us to be. And he did it by means of Jesus*
> *Christ. (Romans 3:23, The Message Bible)*

Jesus died for the sins of everyone. That includes every man and woman, boy and girl, every nationality and every economic level. Christ died for our specific individual shortcomings as well as the sin that plagues our corrupt world. From a toddling child to an aged man on his deathbed, no one is beyond reach of our Savior:

> *This is how much God loved the world: He gave*
> *his Son, his one and only Son. And this is why:*
> *so that no one need be destroyed; by believing in*
> *him, anyone can have a whole and lasting life.*
> *God didn't go to all the trouble of sending his*
> *Son merely to point an accusing finger, telling the*
> *world how bad it was. He came to help, to put the*
> *world right again. Anyone who trusts in him is*
> *acquitted...(John 3:16-18, The Message Bible)*

Jesus Forgives. All sin is forgiven and every vile act covered by the work of Christ on the cross. In God's unending mercy, He promises to pardon us and remove the effects of our failures:

> *Blessed are they whose transgressions are forgiven, whose sins are covered. Blessed is the man whose sin the Lord will never count against him. Romans 4:7-8*

The way back to God has been paved by a loving son right into the heart of his Heavenly Father. You are forgiven! His love has accepted you and washed away the effects of worldly living.

Salvation Is Not Earned. A friend once told me "I'll be glad to go to church with you as soon as I clean up my act." That's putting the cart before the horse! We cannot prepare ourselves for God. It is a come-as-you-are invitation! He is the one who does the cleaning up.

No one can earn God's salvation—it is a gift from His heart. There is nothing that qualifies us for this gift and nothing that disqualifies us from receiving it. Salvation is a long-awaited present that we need only take and unwrap:

> *Saving is all his idea, and all his work. All we do is trust him enough to let him do it. It's God's gift from start to finish! We don't play the major role.*

If we did, we'd probably go around bragging that we'd done the whole thing! No, we neither make nor save ourselves. God does both the making and saving. (Ephesians 2:8-9, The Message Bible)

You Are a New Creature. Jesus infuses us with life. His power destroys our old patterns of living. A new longing to know God and walk in His ways replaces our selfish desires:

Therefore, if anyone is in Christ, he is a new creation; the old has gone, the new has come! (2 Corinthians 5:17)

Our new inheritance means we have the rights and privileges that were once in the Garden of Eden. *Kainos* is the Greek word for "new" in this passage. It means "new, fresh, unworn, different from the usual, better than the old, superior in value or attraction." Salvation offers a fresh start, a chance for a new beginning and a better way of life according to God's intentions.

The original word for "has gone" is *parerchormai* and means "to pass away, come to an end, disregard, and especially to enter into an inheritance." As far as God is concerned, what has happened in the past is now left in the past. The slate is wiped clean and everything will be different.

Jesus is Alive. The grave sites of spiritual leaders

like Mohammad, Buddha, and Confucius are shrines to their philosophies and belief systems. Their respective tombs are filled with decaying earthly remains.

Unlike these men, Jesus distinguished Himself by leaving much more than godly principles to follow. You may visit the crucifixion site and tour the place where he was entombed, but his remains cannot be found.

Jesus died, was buried, and then resurrected by the power of God! His body did not decay. He is just as alive today as he was thousands of years ago. This one resounding fact distinguishes Christianity from all other religions…we serve a living Savior!

> *I am the First and the Last. I am the Living One; I was dead, and behold I am alive for ever and ever! And I hold the keys of death and Hades. (Revelation 1:17-18)*

These truths are the good seed planted within our spirits. But they expose a few of the many possible weeds that could be growing. Did you discover any weeds? Uproot them by asking for forgiveness, rejecting the lies, and believing the truth of the gospel message.

The Work of the Holy Spirit

The Father, Son, and Holy Spirit celebrate the process of watching us mature. God has already provided everything that we require for healthy and sustainable growth.

God has designed a destiny for us, a perfect plan for our success and fulfillment.

He has given us an identity, a direct deposit of Himself which resides in our spiritual and physical DNA.

He has equipped us with authority, an opportunity to demonstrate the rule of God in our sphere of influence.

He has placed us within a community of believers so that we are nurtured and loved.

And finally, God has promised that He would provide for us. He is all sufficient in every realm of our life.

But, let's not stop there.

We haven't been left on our own to figure out the path forward. When Jesus left the earthly realm, he spoke to his disciples and told them this:

> *But I tell you the truth: It is for your good that I am going away. Unless I go away, the Counselor will not come to you; but if I go, I will send him to you. (John 16:7)*

Jesus was referring to the Holy Spirit, the one who will counsel and guide us in the days to come. He is known by many names throughout the Bible: the Comforter, the Spirit of Truth, the Counselor, the Helper.

The Holy Spirit now lives in us and will be with us every step of our journey. He will lead and guide. He will teach, encourage, and strengthen.

The Holy Spirit carries on the role of Master Gardener over his planting. He oversees our Christian growth:

> *And I (Jesus) will ask the Father, and he will give you another Counselor to be with you forever— the Spirit of truth. The world cannot accept him, because it neither sees him nor knows him. But you know him, for he lives with you and will be in you...But the Counselor, the Holy Spirit, whom the Father will send in my name, will teach you all things and will remind you of everything I have said to you. (John 14:16, 17,26)*

As we cooperate with the Holy Spirit, we experience the vital spiritual relationship that Jesus enjoyed. It is the Holy Spirit who explains all things, gives counsel, and directs our life. As we learn to follow, we have the assurance that we are on the right path.

Moving Forward in Faith

Where do we begin? How can we cooperate with God as he directs our spiritual journey? The following steps will help move you forward in your journey of faith:

1. Ask God to guide you to a church. Attend regularly and take notice of the changes in your life.

2. Plug into a local Bible study or small group. Learn more about this spiritual adventure you have begun.

3. Uproot any false concepts of God. Rely on the truth of the Bible as your standard for living.

4. Find a Bible that you understand. You may select from many versions. The New International Version and the Message Bible are two translations used in this book.

5. Spend time daily with God. Pray...read your Bible...worship the Lord with songs and music!

6. Invite God's presence into everything. You will discover a forever friend who will never

leave or forsake you.

God has planted you in the soil of His Kingdom.

Take root and grow. Become what God has always destined you to be!

> *They will be called oaks of righteousness,*
> *a planting of the Lord for the display*
> *of his splendor. (Isaiah 61:3)*

Heavenly Father,

Thank you for your plan of salvation. I give you my life and want to grow and mature into the person you designed me to be. I ask for the counsel, comfort, and help of the Holy Spirit. May I be sensitive to his guidance.

Show me the negative areas of my life that could hinder my growth. Expose the lies I have believed, even the half-truths. Help me to walk in your truth.

Please lead me to a place and people where I can be nurtured and grow in you. Where you lead me, I will follow. Thank you, Lord.

Amen

MY GIFT TO YOU!

Established 30 Day Devotional Journal

Download Your FREE Copy at

www.pampalagyi.com

ACKNOWLEDGMENTS

I think it is impossible to create in a vacuum! There are so many people who have contributed their time, opinions, and prayer in this endeavor. Thank you for making this possible!

First of all my family...husband Paul, my daughters Lisa (and husband Crip) and Laurie. Their patience and support is invaluable to me.

My lifelong friend Pat who has been in the trenches with me over decades. You are a gem and know my heart.

Kudos go out to my web designer and website mastermind, Angela McPherson of Netchicks Marketing. You have paved the digital path before me and answered my countless questions graciously.

My church friends and the many more who support my ministry through social media and my website. Your words of encouragement always inspire me to move forward.

Blessings and thanks from a very grateful heart!

You have made this book a reality.

ABOUT THE AUTHOR

My family is the center of my life. My husband Paul works in the aerospace industry and we have two daughters and two granddaughters. Paul and I have traveled life's roads together. We enjoy working around the home, golfing, biking, travel, and a good movie...with lots of popcorn!

Since 1998, I have traveled to five continents equipping and encouraging others in leadership development, personal growth seminars, mentoring, and conferences. I served as a pastor, created and administered three Christian training centers, and mentored rising leaders from around the world.

I hold a Master of Divinity degree from Regent University. My publications include *Established: Seeking God's Plan for Spiritual Growth; Empowered: A Practical Guide for Personal Ministry; The Word Became Flesh: Studies in the Gospel of John; and 7 Easy Steps to Goal Setting Success.*

I am also a contributor to the devotional *Life in the Spirit*, Charles Stanley's *In Touch* magazine, CBN online magazine, and have published various other articles. I study writing and publication process and have become a mentor for other aspiring writers.

For more information about my ministry and resources, connect with me on my website at

www.pampalagyi.com

Sign up for my blog which features posts on leadership, personal growth, writing, and a mix of creative ideas. You can also find me on Facebook, LinkedIn, Twitter, and Instagram.

EMPOWERED: A PRACTICAL GUIDE TO PERSONAL MINISTRY

Empowered is the second book in the Foundation of Faith series. It is a comprehensive, guide for outreach and personal ministry. The guide explains the Biblical foundations that will increase your understanding and strengthen your faith.

Within its pages, you will find practical steps to help in these areas:

- Hearing the voice of God

- Leading Others to Salvation

- Praying for the Baptism of the Holy Spirit

- Healing Prayer

- Deliverance

- Releasing the Blessing of God

Get ready to move beyond the ordinary and into the extraordinary! God is waiting for you to take part in this historic surge of his power. It's time to activate your faith and be empowered for ministry!

The *Empowered Study Guide* is also available for groups or individuals.

THE WORD BECAME FLESH

In this 8 week, in-depth study of the Gospel of John, Pam Palagyi invites you to enter into the culture and history of New Testament times. Experience the Messiah with fresh eyes and apply those spiritual principles to your own life. The study features:

- The seven 'I AM" statements

- The seven signs of the Messiah

- Historical and cultural background

- Word studies and commentary

- Practical applications